LESSER RAILWAYS OF THE YORKSHIRE DALES

AND THE DAM BUILDERS IN THE AGE OF STEAM

HAROLD D BOWTELL

PLATEWAY PRESS

LESSER RAILWAYS OF THE YORKSHIRE DALES

And the Dam Builders in the Age of Steam

by Harold D Bowtell

Plateway Press

Books by the same Author:

Reservoir Railways of Manchester and the Peak
Reservoir Railways of the Yorkshire Pennines
Over Shap to Carlisle – the Lancaster and Carlisle Railway in the 20th Century
Lesser Railways of Bowland Forest and Craven Country
Rails Through Lakeland: Workington – Cockermouth – Keswick – Penrith

British Library Cataloguing in Publication Data

Bowtell, Harold D.
   Lesser railways of the Yorkshire Dales:
   and the dam builders in the age of steam.
   1.   North Yorkshire (England). Reservoirs.
   Construction. Use of Narrow gauge railways, history
   I.   Title
   385.54094284

   ISBN 1-871980-09-7

© Harold D Bowtell 1991

All rights reserved. No part of this publication may be reproduced, stored in a retrieval system, or transmitted, in any form or by any means, electronic, mechanical or photocopying, recording or otherwise, without the prior permission of the Publisher.

Printed in Great Britain by Amadeus Press Ltd, Huddersfield

Front cover illustration: Manning Wardle 0-4-0ST XIT, on mixed gauge yard tracks at Lofthouse (Nidd Valley Light Railway), takes a 'peek' at ex-Metropolitan Railway 4-4-0T and stock, on trial for the Railway's opening, around 1906–7. (Sketch by Michael Blackmore.)

Contents

		Page
	Preface	5
Chapter 1	Leeds in the Washburn valley and at Eccup – opening of the era of constructional railways	7
Chapter 2	Harrogate at Scargill and Roundhill – and Leeds enters Colsterdale	15
Chapter 3	Leeds in Colsterdale	33
Chapter 4	Locomotives in Colsterdale	47
Chapter 5	Kirkby Malzeard Light Railway	63
Chapter 6	Transport by City Tramways	65
Chapter 7	Reservoirs and Railways for the City of Bradford	70
Chapter 8	Upper Barden reservoir	73
Chapter 9	Railways and reservoirs in the upper valley of the Nidd	76
Chapter 10	Haden Carr dam and the aqueduct to Bradford – Morrison & Mason Ltd	79
Chapter 11	Chellow Heights reservoirs – Phineas Drake, contractor	84
Chapter 12	Gouthwaite reservoir – John Best & Son, Edinburgh	84
Chapter 13	Forward to Angram, 1900–1904	86
Chapter 14	Angram reservoir – John Best & Son/John Best & Sons Ltd	91
Chapter 15	The Nidd Valley Light Railway – its earlier days	101
Chapter 16	The Scar House era, 1913–1936	115
Chapter 17	Railway operation in Scar House days, 1921–1936	133
Chapter 18	Locomotives in Nidderdale, distinguishing John Best and the Corporation of Bradford	139
	Water from the Yorkshire Dales: addendum	157
	Acknowledgments	159

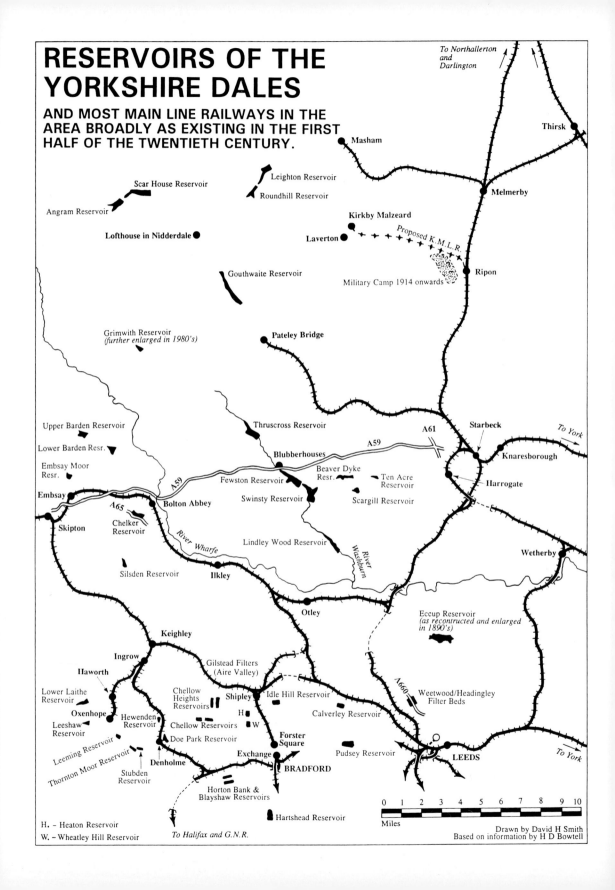

Preface

My account of building dams and creating reservoirs in Britain during the 'age of steam' (circa 1870–1940) – with railways and their people central to the story – has already run through three volumes: in sequence, *Manchester and the Peak*, *Yorkshire Pennines*, *Bowland Forest and Craven Country*. Now, the object is to explore the 'Yorkshire Dales' northward of Leeds and Bradford and re-create the projects undertaken for Leeds, Harrogate and Bradford. I recommend: first take a look at the territory, as displayed by our map of the overall territory embraced.

In the north, Masham village, Leighton and Roundhill reservoirs are seen, linked loosely by Colsterdale. I first came on Colsterdale one icy January morning in the 1950s. It took two of us to help Bill Young's small car up the more slippery slopes between Leeds and the Dale. There, the scene was breathtaking in the snow. Repeated tramps thereabouts were mainly in the years to 1963, with a preliminary account presented in the Journal of the Stephenson Locomotive Society, May 1964. While adding since then to documentary back-up and much other clarification, it has also been a joy to revisit sites in the dale, and find friends old and new, also visiting Harrogate's Scargill and the valleys of the Washburn and the Wharfe, down to the northern outskirts of Leeds. The *main* period researched was 1901–1926.

Acknowledgments are recorded at the close of this book. Bear in mind that everyone mentioned in that crowded page is an individual who has willingly provided personal help, anecdote, information or illustration, many becoming firm friends. I aim to convey something of their knowledge and enthusiasms, and to pay tribute to the many sadly no longer with us. Even my long-time friend and cartographic colleague Arthur Chambers has passed on, since he saw with delight the production of *Bowland and Craven*; however most of the maps and diagrams now presented were drawn by Arthur.

In Colsterdale, Teddy Mills, at Fearby, was one of the great figures who had enjoyed a lifetime among steam locomotives employed in the 'public works' of the hills. He compared with Charlie Chambers who is featured in the dedication to my *Reservoir Railways of the Yorkshire Pennines*. I believe that for years Teddy was a focus of attention at the annual Pateley show (or 'feast'), when 'public works' folk came together from all over Britain to relive old times *and* tell one another of jobs current or in prospect.

Turning to Nidderdale, my first peep was in company with Arthur Camwell, in 1935, at Pateley Bridge, viewing North Eastern Railway station and activity – and within and without the Bradford Corporation's station, layouts, engine and carriage sheds; there were still engines, railcar and passenger stock from the preceding years: 1890–1935.

This is my opportunity to stress the distinction between the activities – and locomotives – of the City of Bradford's several public works contractors and their own work by direct labour. The City's statutory Nidd Valley Light Railway was shorter in time and miles, and in many ways subsidiary to the whole conception and achievement in upper Nidderdale. This theme is developed in the text.

Pateley Bridge is a charming spot today but – dare I say – it was even more delightful when one came by the Saturdays Only business train from Bradford Forster Square station to Harrogate and onwards by the branch train from Harrogate to Pateley. This ideally led to a leisurely walk over the link line to Corporation territory, and exploration for some dozen miles beyond. These were rough miles in the days described, back to 1890, and even during my travels of 1960–72 the upper dale was remote. Today, all – well, nearly all – of those upper miles are accessible to motor car, though not motor coach.

Upper Nidderdale associates for me with tramps in company of Arthur Chambers but also Stuart Rankin and then that grand character Thomas Garth, whose vivid memories from working days at Scar House were aroused by Stuart and myself; Tommy Garth proceeded to delve for pictures until his regretted death in June 1976. George Renton had known all the Scar House construction era as an engineer on site in the 1920s and 1930s, and then moved to be chief engineer of Bradford Water based at their city head office; in retirement, he came out up the dale with enthusiasm, and professional interpretation withal. There was an engineer colleague in George Renton's time at Scar House who was also an artist of distinction. This was David Rose, whom I never met. His daughter Margaret Rose has filled out the story of their days in the unique village at Scar House. Many of the Rose pictures are held in the art collections of Harrogate and Bradford and may be viewed on occasion. I have been privileged to produce evocative samples of his work, sketches made available by Bradford Water from their collection. A session with Humphrey Household, then in Perthshire, brought the story of his Saturday afternoon cycling trips in the 1920s, when he was a young and keen 'traffic apprentice' of the London & North Eastern Railway, based at York. A group of his pictures is produced in appreciation. More may be secured by acquiring his recent reminiscent book on minor railways visited.

Locomotive lore came from many firesides, but not all in the West Riding! Exploring the course and history of the Cork, Blackrock and Passage Railway in Ireland, twenty years ago, what fun it was to come upon Jack Murphy, at his home above Monkstown, County Cork. Jack, at age 12 years, in 1901, had joined Edinburgh contractor John Best there on the coast. He told, inter alia, of 3ft gauge locomotive TULLIBARDINE (see my piece in the book on John Best locomotives in upper Nidderdale) and how its driver Paddy Woods was always accompanied by his dog, seated on the cab roof – limpet like on that modest appendage, I would think – while his master's locomotive shifted 'muck' in the making of Monkstown cutting. Great friends who continue to fill out and interpret individual locomotive histories include Geoff Horsman, with a career in industrial locomotive design and building, and Allan Baker as one of British Railways' most travelled and experienced locomotive engineers, maybe looking now towards Tunnel motive power.

Kendal, Westmorland
March, 1991

Harold D Bowtell

Publisher's Note

The books *Reservoir Railways of Manchester and the Peak* and *Reservoir Railways of the Yorkshire Pennines* referred to by the author in this Preface are out of print. *Lesser Railways of Bowland Forest and Craven Country* is (1991) in print and can be obtained from Plateway Press: see back jacket flap for more information.

It is regretted that copies of photographs featured in the book cannot be supplied to individuals.

Chapter One

Leeds in the Washburn Valley and at Eccup – Opening of the Era of Constructional Railways

Pre-history

The organised search for water for Leeds dates back at least to 1790, when the Commissioners of the Leeds Water Works secured their first Act. In 1837 the Leeds Waterworks Company was created and by the eighteen-fifties water from the river Wharfe was being piped to a storage reservoir, capacity 257 million gallons, at Eccup, on the high ground some five miles north of the town; and just to westward there were small reservoirs on the Adel beck. Leeds Corporation took over by Act of 1852 and, authorised by Acts of 1856 and 1862, employed steam pumping plant at Arthington to abstract water from the Wharfe. Their Act of 1867 permitted a major development in the Washburn valley; in course of this project, 1869–80, steam plant was widely employed and steam railway working introduced. Consultants were Thomas Hawksley of Westminster and Edward Filliter of Leeds. Direct labour was employed under Mr Bower (the Corporation's manager at Lindley Wood) and, after a spell assisting at Lindley Wood, Robert Brooks was appointed manager at Swinsty and Fewston.

The Skipton to Harrogate moorland road (A59) crosses the Washburn at Blubberhouses and the project included the creation of three principal reservoirs in the seven miles of the valley south eastwards to its emergence into the Wharfe, about two miles downstream from Otley. Each of these reservoirs involved an earth dam with puddle clay core, the lowest being at Lindley Wood and its construction was tackled first.

Lindley Wood, 1869–1876: top water level 299ft, capacity 750 million gallons

The local landowner, to whose views the Leeds Corporation deferred on various aspects, was Mr Fawkes, of Leathley Hall, and clay for the subsidiary dam at Washburn Foot (1874–76) came from his land. For the main dam, Lindley Wood, the implications are that the same source was used or that suitable clay was found within the actual site. The embankment would be formed from earthfill dug manually, before the days of 'steam navvies'. Most of the stone required was from Farnley Crag quarry, to west of the embankment. There was difficulty in finding a contractor to work the quarry and by 1871 Mr Bower was himself employing the gangs. Stone was brought down by carts, using a road which passed through the farm of Mr Doggett and this continued until about the end of 1876. Imported supplies were carted from Otley station. Steam railways were not employed on site but there were 3ft gauge tracks, using 26 pounds per yard rail (believed iron rails). Railway tip wagons were made in the site workshop, with wheels, axles and iron fittings bought in (pivots and angle plates are referred to by interested visitors from Huddersfield), at a cost of about £4.6.0d per wagon, to which is added the price of timber, carpentry and assembly. The first sod was cut on 23 August 1869 and, with work on site at its peak, the Huddersfield visitors of February 1871 found 41 horses employed and about 400 men. The cut-off trench across the valley on the dam centre line had been excavated and was being filled with clay, four steam engine driven pugmills being worked night and day and on Sundays during that winter and into the ensuing spring.

Other supporting plant included carts, barrows, various steam engines driving items such as saw bench and stone breaker. There were cranes handling masonry in the quarry and at site.

The workshops were near the bywash, to the north of the embankment site. Offices and stores were close to the south end of the bank. The workmen's huts were near the Glaston beck, probably on the south west edge of the eventual reservoir. The timekeeper's hut was close by the manager's house – a stone house, presumably part of a farm, demolished towards the end of 1875. This in turn was prudently within sight of the men's quarters. Two West Riding policemen had a living hut and there were the occasional incidents, as when T Kirkham, driver of No. 14 cart, was found drunk on duty and dismissed and Thomas Booth of No. 11 cart was cautioned.

The site provision shop was run by a contractor, initially John Deighton of Leeds, but with two later changes of tenancy. The sale of beer was restricted to a half hour at breakfast time, one hour at dinner time and between 5.30 and 8.0 in the evening. The navvies had a discerning palate for beer. Initially the Corporation bought it at 1/–d to 1/2d per gallon and sold it at 2½d per pint but there were vociferous complaints as to quality. By August 1872 all contending brews had been tested (by the navvies) and found wanting, except the products of Tetley & Company, Leeds; these were then bought at 1/–d per gallon (mild ale) and 1/6d per gallon (bitter) and the latter retailed at 6d per quart (namely ¼ gallon or 2 pints).

Mr Constable (a local clergyman) was from the start most concerned that beer should not be sold to local residents; he referred to 'the temptation of the beer house' and the possible demoralisation of his rural population. Mr S R Anderson, Vicar of Otley, sought fifty per cent contribution by the Corporation to the £150 annual stipend of a curate 'to labour amongst the navigators' but the waterworks committee declined to contribute. In August 1870, various employees approached the Mayor of Leeds, seeking a site for a church and school. By November, a room (no doubt a hut) was provided for public worship and a school was set up at Lindley Wood. However, in April 1871, the school premises were commandeered in emergency as a temporary smallpox hospital, as the Otley Guardians had failed to equip the barn set aside for the purpose of an isolation hospital. Later, a cottage at Hill Syke, near Fewston, was adapted as the hospital.

In February 1872, the corporation acceded to the workers' demands for 'the nine hours system', work to begin at 7.0 a.m. On Saturdays it was to end at 2.0 p.m., but the managers were given authority to concede a 1.0 p.m. finish on Saturdays, if necessary to avoid a strike.

Although steam power on rails does not seem to have been considered, the possibility of acquiring a Thompson's road 'steamer' was raised in March 1870. This would be an upright boiler road locomotive on three wheels, of a design by Tennant & Company, of Leith, near Edinburgh. Councillor Craven and Engineer Mr Filliter were deputed to visit Aberdeen to inspect such a locomotive at work in that town and establish its cost of operation. Following their report, the decision went against purchase.

Completion at Lindley Wood was around the end of 1876 and in January 1877 Mr Bower, the site manager, left to manage new construction works at Hull docks.

Swinsty, 1871–1877: top water level 449ft, capacity 960 million gallons

A water mill in the valley was dismantled in February 1871 and some of its materials were used in building huts at Swinsty, which is located northwards from Lindley Wood. In spring 1872, a hut was adapted as a school and the committee advertised for a school-mistress, who would be paid £1 per week; however, hut residents and other married workmen were called upon to accept a deduction of sixpence per week towards this salary. From a labour force of about 300 men, the Corporation would seemingly recover most of their outgo.

Facilities and site plant were basically comparable with those at Lindley Wood but the railhead was at Starbeck on the North Eastern Railway's Leeds Northern line; with a generally uphill haul from there for imports, predominantly coal and cement, the waterworks committee were convinced by Mr Eddison (presumably of the family later well known for hire of steam plant and equipment) that they required a steam traction engine. In April 1871, they ordered from John Fowler's Steam Plough Works, Leeds a 12 horse-power engine; it would be a very powerful road locomotive, comparable with contemporary ploughing engines. The order specified 'without India rubber tyres' and the price was £520. An order for nine wagons for haulage by the engine followed on 1 May 1871. Already, by September 1871, the engine was cutting up the 'Township roads' disastrously and it was decided to use it only on the 'Turnpike road' (A59) and to form a depot, probably at Dangerous Corner, as a reference has been found to making good the fence there; the goods were to be unloaded at the depot and taken forward over the by-roads ('Township roads') by horse and cart. Soon, the office of the Harrogate Commissioners was transmitting complaints of the smoke nuisance in the vicinity of that spa, so coke was substituted for coal, but the Trustees of the Skipton and Knaresborough Road (the 'Turnpike') had by now awakened to the damage being done on the route from Starbeck. On 15 January 1872, the Leeds Corporation succumbed and the traction engine was stopped, all materials henceforth to be carted from Starbeck to Swinsty by contractors.

Railway tip wagons for 3ft gauge were again built and 30 pounds per yard iron rails were secured early in 1873. There was a railway incline down from Swinsty quarry to the site and probably this was the incline for which in April 1874 a wire rope ¾in diameter and 220 yards long was ordered from John Fowler & Company. Incidentally, the Fowler traction engine of 1871 had been supplied complete with a clip for drum pulleys and steel rope. Maybe it could anchor itself and wind its road wagons up steep pitches and perhaps it subsequently took up permanent duty on the quarry railway incline at Swinsty.

In June 1873, Leeds waterworks committee ordered their first railway locomotive, from Manning Wardle of Leeds; the 3ft gauge locomotive WASHBURN, being a 0-4-0 Saddle tank with 6in x 12in cylinders, which arrived at Swinsty in October 1873. It is not known whether it hauled stone from incline foot to crusher or worked primarily on site haulage of trucks of clay or 'fill' for the embankment. Incidentally, dobbin carts were used at Swinsty and they would be for tipping 'fill' to form the embankment.

A second 3ft gauge steam locomotive came in September 1875. This was AMALGAMATION, 0-4-0 Saddle tank with 8in x 14in cylinders, Hunslet 102, acquired second-hand but only two years old from Huddersfield Corporation's waterworks above the Colne valley and consigned via Meltham station. It may have worked for a time at Swinsty, before going on to the nearby Fewston site.

The work at Swinsty was about finished in January 1877, when various huts were removed and filling of the reservoir commenced. Surplus plant from Lindley Wood and Swinsty (but not the two railway locomotives) was offered for sale by auction around June 1877.

Fewston, 1874–1879: top water level 503ft, capacity 866 million gallons

This is the topmost reservoir built in the Washburn valley in the eighteen-seventies, with its head 'touching' the turnpike road at Blubberhouses. Work began around July 1874, utilising some of the plant released from Lindley Wood and Fewston, including 3ft gauge railway wagons and, one presumes, the two steam railway locomotives already referred to; these went on to the Corporation's Eccup site on completion at Fewston. Stone came from Mr McConochie's quarry above Fewston (at 2/6d per square yard) and from Mr Bramley's quarry at Swinsty Hall at 1/–d per square yard, but no hint has been found that a Corporation incline or railway working was employed for the stone, except that it is known that a 300 yards long haulage rope was required for a railway incline for getting of earth for the embankment at Fewston!

Fewston mill was demolished early in the job and its waterwheels and machinery advertised. West Houses mills at Blubberhouses were pulled down about 1877–78 and stone from them was used to build the permanent wall round Fewston reservoir, but the two West Houses villas, which were let by the Corporation, were not to be pulled down. At the end, in June 1880, a row of cottages near Blubberhouses bridge and Fewston reservoir was demolished; no doubt they were used to accommodate staff or navvies during the job.

The permanent sluice valves were closed on 20 October 1879 and water impounded. On Monday 3 November 1879, the supply valves for water to Leeds were opened for the first time, by the Mayor – with a golden key – supported by the Corporation and Mr Hawksley, the senior consulting engineer for the whole project in the valley.

Robert Brooks had secured a useful salary for the day, £350 per annum, when in July 1874 he was appointed to manage the Fewston construction works as well as Swinsty. However, he was in trouble in March 1875 when he had to admit to having been seen intoxicated and driving furiously between Otley and Swinsty in the cart provided by the committee for his use when on business. Nevertheless, he retained the confidence of the committee and in August 1879 was desired to take charge at Eccup during the building of a new service reservoir there. Samuel Brooks then lived in the cottage at Fewston to oversee the completion of the works.

A tragic episode was reported on 17 June 1878. John Cook, a navvy known as 'Mad Stafford', was dismissed nine weeks previously from the Fewston workforce on account of violent conduct. He went on to attempt murder and then committed suicide at Fewston. Navvies were often nicknamed after the scenes of their earlier exploits and one visualises this unfortunate fellow toiling for the famous railway contractors Brassey and Field in building the Stafford and Uttoxeter Railway (later Great Northern Railway) circa 1865–67.

Thruscross: the long-delayed sequel in the Washburn valley

As Lindley Wood's top water level is only about 300ft o.d. and it was committed from the beginning to supply of 'compensation water' to the possessors of riparian rights, the construction of three dams, 1869–79, produced no more than 1825 million gallons of impounded supply for the citizens of Leeds. Thus, it is not surprising that the Corporation sought to construct a higher-level reservoir in the valley. In 1896, North Corner farm at West End, Thruscross – north of Fewston and Blubberhouses – was purchased, and let on six months' notice. Acquisition of farms in the vicinity continued in 1897–99, also (in 1898) the Gate Inn and the Smith's Arms, both at Fewston and each with blacksmith's shop and other buildings and cottages. There were designs on lands of the Duke of Devonshire and Lord Walsingham and a Bill was drafted to authorise removal of the Holy Trinity Church, Thruscross (West End) and its burial ground.

If the works had proceeded in early twentieth century, one might have looked for the use of steam diggers and reservoir railways, but the interest of Leeds turned to the country above Masham. Thruscross dam was eventually constructed in 1961–66, well after our 'age of steam' in public works. The top water level is 710ft o.d. and capacity 1725 million gallons.

Eccup New Reservoir, 1879–1885: top water level 377ft, capacity 1331 m.g.

It was decided to enlarge the early storage reservoir, existing capacity 257 million gallons, at Eccup, immediately north of Leeds. Under an Act of 1877, a new embankment was to be built and the old one removed. Lands were purchased from Lord Harewood, the site being on the southern edge of the Harewood House estate, and from Mr George Lane Fox. The consulting engineer was Edward Filliter, of Leeds, and no reference to Mr Hawksley has been traced during the actual period of construction – which was by direct labour under Robert Brooks, transferred from Fewston as the Corporation's site manager. He took possession of Alwoodley New Hall (a farmhouse); it was vacated by Mrs Brooks in April 1883 following her husband's sudden death. James Townsend, Corporation foreman on site, was accommodated at Goodrick House; he took full charge in 1883–84 after Mr Brooks's death. The first sod was turned on 29 September 1879 and a dinner followed at the Queen's Hotel, Leeds.

There was no main line railway connection and imported materials came to site by road, with access via Eccup village (to the north west) and thence by an accommodation road on the Harewood estate, believed to be the private road which parallels the north shore of the reservoir. The dam was (and is) at the east end of the site and a working area hereabouts was rented from Lord Harewood during 1879–83. Coal, cement, bricks, plant, etc were brought into this area. Stone probably came from the Sturdy Beck quarry of Mr Moorson; if this was eastward of the site, the mode of access is not clear, as the present east end waterworks approach road from the Leeds–Harrogate main road was constructed later, in 1882–83. The offices and stables were at the west end of the site, near the road access from Eccup village. A hut for scripture readers was accepted as a gift from Miss Heaton and this was erected near Alwoodley Old Hall, namely to the south of the site, implying that a workers' village was built in that area. *Building News* reported that 400–500 men were employed at the peak of the job.

Considerable railway material was used. Some was probably brought from Fewston and recourse was had to a sale at Gisburn station on 27–28 April, 1881; this was the sale of plant of T J Waller, contractor, on completion of building the Lancashire and Yorkshire Railway's Chatburn to Hellifield extension. About another mile of track materials were bought in 1881–82 and, when in August 1882 the time came to remove the old dam embankment, the 3ft gauge railway layout on site was extended and the locomotive SPONDON and twenty-five additional side-tipping wagons were acquired frorm Benton and Woodiwiss, contractors for Manchester waterworks, at Guide Bridge. Until then, the two locomotives from Fewston had sufficed. When *Building News* reported in May 1883 that work was nearing completion at Eccup, they recorded that three locomotives were in use – which reconciles with the number traced as being available. Probably all their work was towards the easterly end of the site, in forming the new bank and handling puddle clay, and removing the old bank, including moving its material for use in completing the new dam.

As early as May 1882, during rapid filling of the puddle trench in the new reservoir embankment, an unusual amount of settlement was noted. The job was essentially finished in October 1883 and steam cranes, locomotives and large plant were offered for sale from then onwards; the three locomotives appear to have been sold during the first quarter of 1884. Filling was somewhat delayed, but achieved by 15 March 1885.

Reconstruction of Eccup New Reservoir, 1889–1898

The construction of this reservoir occupied about five years with, as already remarked, up to 500 men employed. It was at once in trouble. Excessive settlement of the embankment occurred, accompanied by major leakage; in August 1888, the loss was over 700,000 gallons per day. It took over eight years' hard work to put it right.

One senses that the Hawksleys were in disfavour and Mr Filliter was only called upon when peremptorily required from time to time to produce drawings of the works. The consultant retained for the duration of the reconstruction was the eminent George H Hill, of Manchester, whose firm continued the Bateman tradition. After investigation, George Hill and the borough engineer, Mr Hewson, agreed that water was passing through fissures in the rock upon which the shallow southerly portion of the puddle-clay core was based; that this portion of the puddle wall must be taken down to the same depth as the northerly portion, namely somewhere between 150 and 158ft from the top of the wall (that is, more or less, the top of the embankment) to its foundation on the rock well below ground level. It might also be necessary to construct a wing trench at the south east end of the embankment. In the event, the wing trench proved unnecessary but *the whole length* of the clay core had to be removed and its bottom taken down deeper and the whole refilled. To an extent, the material of the embankment itself had to be shifted and reinstalled, as the depth of the excavation within the core and trench was too great to be timbered from top to bottom whilst devoid of clay; the timber would be subject to great crushing stress and collapse of timbering imperils lives.

The digging out of the clay was done in three stages, by contractors –
1. Southern portion, by Gould & Stevenson, of Hunslet, circa November 1889 to September 1892.
2. Centre portion, by Isaac Gould, of Hunslet (the partnership having by now been dissolved), circa February 1893 to March 1895.
3. Northern portion, by Isaac Gould, circa April 1895 to September 1896.

The depth achieved was 174–180ft from top to new foundations. Partial refilling with concrete had been proposed but Mr Hill decided to refill entirely with puddle clay and this was done, each portion in turn, by the Corporation's direct labour under their engineer. In October 1897, Mr Hill authorised refilling of the reservoir and this was accomplished progressively between May and October 1898, without significant leakage; a cure had been achieved but at a cost of £54,000 for contractors, plus much direct labour, supervision and frustration. Later, in October 1914, there was investigation of leakage at Eccup, four boreholes being authorised.

In August–September 1890, Gould & Stevenson were allowed to erect huts on the site to accommodate some of their workmen, in order to increase their workforce. Their work was probably all very local to the embankment and mainly digging out and movement of clay and earthfill; reference has been traced (in 1890) to their use of travelling cranes on excavation. The only specific reference located to steam railway working is the purchase by Gould of one new steam locomotive in 1895, by which time the last portion of the work was in hand. It is on record that Isaac Gould, resident at Westfield Terrace, Chapeltown, Leeds, died in September 1903.

During the first stage of the works, in November 1890, Lord Harewood's solicitors wrote strongly from London to Sir G Morrison, Town Clerk of Leeds, to complain that dirty water was being pumped from the Eccup site into the beck and injuring the ornamental waters in Harewood Park. His Lordship had engaged Mr G F Deacon, the engineer to the Liverpool Corporation and noted for his work at Vyrnwy, to inspect the alleged damage and advise.

Locomotives

Locomotives, 3ft gauge, of Leeds Corporation, at Swinsty, Fewston and Eccup New Reservoir

WASHBURN   0-4-0 Saddle tank oc 6in x 12in
by Manning Wardle 478 of 1873, ordered 6/1873 and new ex works 17/10/1873 to Leeds Corporation at Swinsty;
design based on 2ft 6in gauge loco MW 97 but 'extensively altered', including as to gauge.
It worked for Leeds at Swinsty, Fewston and Eccup; and for sale early 1884.
Subsequently with Little Orme's Head Limestone Company, Llandudno (this being makers' intelligence) and believed named LITTLE ORME. Later again (from 1914?) with Ship Canal Portland Cement Manufacturers Company, at their Ellesmere Port Works (again, makers' information).

AMALGAMATION   0-4-0 Saddle tank oc 8in x 14in
by Hunslet 102 of 1873 – had been new to Huddersfield Corporation (see page B25 in *Yorkshire Pennines*) and acquired thence 9/1875 by Leeds for Swinsty, Fewston and Eccup; and for sale early 1884. Subsequently with Walter Scott & Company, who used it as COTHERSTONE on their Hury and Blackton reservoir contracts in Baldersdale, circa 1884–91; the loco was replaced by a new COTHERSTONE around 1891.

SPONDON   0-4-0 Saddle tank oc 9in x 14in
by Hunslet 208 of 1878 – had been new to Benton & Woodiwiss (*Manchester and the Peak*, page 19) and acquired from them at Guide Bridge circa 10/1882 for use by Leeds Corporation at Eccup; and for sale 1/1884.
Subsequently with Charles Baker & Sons of Chesterfield and probably on their Moss Moor catchwater construction of circa 1883–88, feeding Ringstone reservoir (pages B67–70 in *Yorkshire Pennines*).
Proceeded from Baker to Ireland circa 29/5/1891 (makers' date) – or possibly a little earlier as it is believed to have been on construction of the southern portion of what we have known as the West Clare Railway, opened 1892 (W Murphy, contractor?). Later again, with James Nuttall of Manchester on building the Lynton and Barnstaple Railway in Devon (job of 1895–98) and in Trafford Park (?building the three miles Trafford Park Tramway, Barton to Royal Show entrance, circa 1897–98).
Finally, associated with the name of Smith and Pass.
A possible first owner of this loco in Ireland has been suggested. Collen Brothers (Cavan & Leitrim Railway construction works of 1886–88) offered a 9in cylinder 3ft gauge locomotive by Hunslet Engine Company for sale in Ireland (*Contract Journal* 23/1/1889); however, it is understood by a good authority that the Collens had their relevant loco by 3/1887 and that it was called VICTOR, and could not be our SPONDON.

Locomotive, 3ft gauge, of Isaac Gould, presumed at Eccup when new

HANNAH	0-4-0 Saddle tank oc 9in x 16in

by Black Hawthorn of Gateshead, 1125 of probably 1895; ordered 16/8/1895, 'for delivery on rail at Leeds in 8–10 weeks' – the makers quoted the purchaser as Isaac Gould, builder and brick maker, of Hartshead Works, Hillidge Road, Leeds. Presumably, delivered to Eccup and seemingly used by Gould in building a mental hospital at Burley-in Wharfedale.

It went back to the makers and then had a later history with Douglas Corporation (West Baldwin reservoir in the Isle of Man); P Drake & Son (Ogden reservoir for Bury); and Sir Robert McAlpine (Alwen reservoir in Wales).

An "official" photo of SPONDON (HE 208/78) used at Eccup during 1882–1884. The nameplate shows the name of her original owner Benton & Woodiwiss, but this may be specially painted in for the photo.

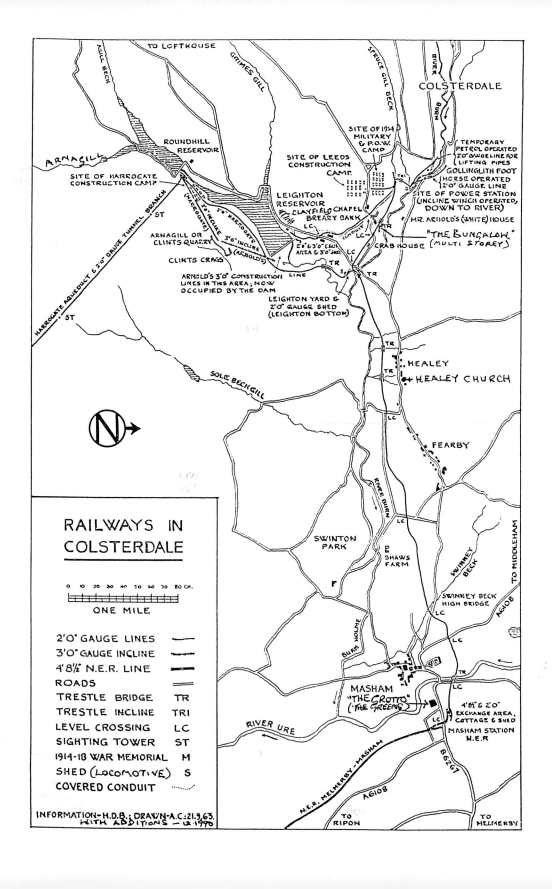

Chapter Two

Harrogate at Scargill and Roundhill – and Leeds enters Colsterdale

Introduction to Harrogate

Water supplies for the town of Harrogate were developed by a private Company, formed in 1846 and reformed in 1860. It was bought out by the borough under the Harrogate Corporation (Waterworks Transfer) Act 1897, effective 1898. Edward Wilson Dixon (like his father before him) was consulting engineer of the Harrogate Waterworks Company and in 1897 he was appointed borough water engineer to the Corporation of Harrogate.

After the very small John o' Gaunt reservoir (25 million gallons at top water level of 567ft o.d.), three more impounding reservoirs were built in Haverah Park, a few miles west of the town. All have earth dams, with clay cores, and they are –

Ten Acres – capacity 31 m.g. at 609ft, built 1867–73 by Thomas Jackson contractor.
Beaver Dyke – capacity 110 m.g. at 559ft, built 1876–c. 1881 by Thomas Jackson contractor.
Scargill – capacity 192 m.g. at 644ft, built 1898–1903 by direct labour.

A service reservoir at Harlow Park, nearer the town, was built by Jackson in 1870–71.

The Scargill project was from the start under the control of E W Dixon, with E B Wright and Louis Sykes appointed assistants in 1900. G H Hill was the consultant. The job included catchwaters, stone lined, and the outlet pipeline towards Harrogate. Stone and clay were both found locally to the site, on Haverah Park lands of Sir Henry Ingilby. Horses and dobbin carts figured and the only railway seems to have been temporary 2ft gauge tracks, laid down first for pipeline work and then transferred to the catchwaters, where stone had to be handled. There is no suggestion of steam locomotion but a portable steam engine, oil engines (by Hornsby of Grantham), steam boilers and steam cranes were employed. Some of the plant came from Mr Nelson, a then well-known railway contractor, at Harrogate station.

Lodgings for workers were in the countryside and also in huts near the site. There was a licensed canteen and foodstore, with keeper. Entertainments were arranged by the engineer for periodical evenings in winter and summer sports were held. Less happily, in March 1903 there was a sudden outbreak of smallpox, five cases.

The Scargill project sheds interesting light on the Navvy Mission Society. In 1898–99 the Society's headquarters was in Oldham and its principal officials were the Reverend C F Ockford and the Reverend R Grimston (secretary). A mission hut and quarters for the missionary were erected at Scargill and the Society appointed Mr Greenwood as missionary (December 1898), succeeded in turn by Mr Priestley and Mr T H Pickles – who moved on to Roundhill.

Introduction to the dales above Masham – and their railways

The village of Masham is some ten miles north west of Ripon in Yorkshire. Stone built, it sits firmly around its extraordinarily spacious square just above the west bank of the river Ure. Its approach by rail left the Leeds Northern line (Leeds–Hartlepool) of the former North Eastern Railway at Melmerby and was a single track branch line of 7¾ miles, completed 1875, with an intermediate station at Tanfield and its terminus a half mile short of Masham itself and on the opposite side of the river from the village. These were quiet parts and the branch line not surprisingly lost its passenger service from 1 January 1931. The branch closed completely from 11 November 1963. The Leeds Northern line itself closed to passengers, Harrogate–Melmerby–Northallerton, from 6 March 1967; at this date the section north of Melmerby closed finally but it was on 9 October 1969 when the last goods train ran between Melmerby and Starbeck and the route effectively closed southwards from Melmerby.

As the twentieth century opened, Harper's horse wagonette (its hood lowered in a good summer) would still make its peaceful way from Masham village to meet all trains, hoping for a passenger. Soon, however, the folk of Masham and the dales to westward, with the village

Passenger trains ran to Masham, 1875–1930, their two platforms sited to the right. Seen in 1963, although soon to close, the site is little changed. Locomotive D3946 has brought the local goods from Starbeck. The solitary wagon is on the middle one of three parallel roads; this track was extended in 1905 to cross the public roadway and swing left into the meadow beyond, for exchange of traffic with the 2ft gauge line up Colsterdale.

2ft gauge locomotive CLARO is crossing one of the trestle viaducts on the Colsterdale line. The span, and depth below, may indicate a tributary crossing, below Healey village.

communities at Fearby and Healey, were viewing with mixed feelings an upsurge of activity calculated permanently to change the landscape of the upper dale, bringing many men and machines to effect the change – and a delightful light railway which was to have a life of thirty years.

The Corporations of Harrogate and Leeds, each with its own scheme but in collaboration, planned to construct reservoirs and impound the Pennine waters. Acts of 1901 authorised the proposed works, which will be described more fully anon. The Harrogate scheme was somewhat the less ambitious and, unlike that of Leeds, it was started promptly and achieved completion in about ten years. The Harrogate Corporation was to form Roundhill reservoir, at Fairthorne, five miles up the main dales road, which continues beyond Roundhill over the moorland ridge by a route only really adapted for motor vehicles in the nineteen-sixties and which descends a few miles on to Lofthouse of Nidd Valley Light Railway fame.

Railway construction on narrow gauge – mainly by Harrogate Corporation

Harrogate's Act authorised a railway commencing about 3½ miles up the dale from Masham, at Leighton bridge, and running from there to Fairthorne. It was built in 1903, to a gauge of two feet. It started at Leighton plant yard, established by the roadside, headed initially southward to cross the stream by a lofty trestle bridge and then climbed on a more south westerly course along the side of the valley remote from the Lofthouse road and cut along the steep lower slopes of Clints Crags, above the top water level of the reservoir projected by Leeds under the name of Leighton. As the construction of Harrogate's dam was approached, Harrogate's quarry line came down leftwards from the Crags by incline and final zig-zag. The 'main line', about two miles long from Leighton yard, approached the construction site at approximately the level of the eventual crest of the dam, as can be seen today. Likewise, the course of tracks reaching lower levels on the hillside can be seen, downstream of the completed dam. Upstream of the dam, these lower alignments are submerged.

A 2ft gauge branch line ran from the Roundhill vicinity into the northern heading of the 3 miles long straight tunnel which carries the Harrogate water main away to the south east under Masham moor, its alignment marked by the prominent sighting towers, three in number, the middle one (now demolished) at 1178ft on the moors.

The southerly (Carlesmoor) end of the tunnel was served by its own 2ft gauge line. On emerging from the heading, this line continued in the open, on a sinuous course, crossing roads and river by viaducts and passing (in due time) beneath the Leeds pipeline from Leighton; it finished up in a quarry, believed to be Stockwith quarry; this quarry and the railway dated from 1904, on lands of Lord Ripon.

The ubiquitous Arthur Atkinson, of Masham, operated a Mann steam wagon, its sides raised by two deep planks to give increased capacity, between Ripon station yard and Carlesmoor tunnel. Atkinson was also employed by Harrogate to haul imported materials from Masham station goods yard to Leighton yard, using his two steam traction engines, MAJESTIC and another, said to have returned recently from service in the South African war.

Already, in June 1902, the Masham Urban District Council were complaining to Harrogate Corporation that the contractor was parking his traction engines in their market place and they were also demanding extra payment for the use of the roads by heavy loads. Before 1903 was out, the road from Masham station to Leighton bridge had become impassable due to the havoc wrought by the traction engines and it was essential to construct a light railway between these points. Leeds considered promoting a joint Bill with Harrogate but Harrogate were committed to 2ft gauge and Leeds, with more ambitious schemes, wished to have a standard gauge line, so each promoted its own Bill in Parliament. The titles were the Harrogate Waterworks Tramroad Bill and Leeds Corporation (Waterworks) Railway Bill. The Leeds Bill also took in the true Colsterdale valley, north westward from Leighton bridge and yard. The landowner mainly concerned, the Hon S C Lister, agreed with Harrogate on 2ft gauge and the Harrogate Waterworks Tramroad Act 1904 was secured, authorising 4 miles, 4 furlongs on that gauge and with authority in Section 26 to carry workmen, servants and others. The Leeds proposals, being

A multi-span trestle bridge brought the 1905 (extension) line from Masham to join here at 'Leighton Yard' with Harrogate's initial route of 1903 onwards up the dale to Fairthorne and Roundhill reservoir site.

Here is a classic shot of LEEDS No.1 approaching Leighton Yard (and the point where the junction for Colsterdale proper was put in by the Leeds Corporation), pausing on the trestle.

in conflict, were not sanctioned and Leeds waterworks committee reluctantly accepted that they must lay 2ft gauge tracks in Colsterdale proper and on their works and employ running powers over Harrogate's tramroad from Masham station.

Be it noted, when Henry Rofe appeared as a witness for the Leeds Railway Bill before a Committee of the Lords, on 26 April 1904, he referred to Harrogate's 2ft gauge tramway from Leighton Yard to Roundhill as 'that little toy railway'. He added that he had seen photographs of it operating and 'would not like to go round the curves with the timber.'

There seems to have been no real difficulty over what amounted to virtual joint operation of the new section of 'main line', constructed in 1904–05 by Arthur Atkinson. Formal agreement on this topic was reached between the two Corporations in December 1904.

It was also necessary for the Corporations to decide what they required of the North Eastern Railway and it was left to Harrogate to achieve a formal contract with the Railway Company. Meanwhile, in October 1904, the N.E.R. wrote to Harrogate 'as to laying down of a third line on the tramway so that 2ft gauge engines and wagons can be run if necessary direct into the N.E.R. goods yard.' The Railway Company were evidently proposing that 'mixed gauge' (three rails to provide for alternative operation of standard and 2ft gauge locomotives and vehicles) might be laid between the station goods yard at Masham and the proposed traffic exchange yard to be created on the opposite side of the road. Harrogate declined to entertain this proposition. The formal contract achieved with the Railway Company was dated 14 April 1905, 'as to Tramroad and sidings at Masham'. The relevant traffic committee minute of the N.E.R. was dated 13 April 1905. The agreement provided for the extension of the middle one ('No. 9 siding') of the group of three parallel tracks in the station yard, passing through the boundary wall, over the road on the level and into exchange sidings in the meadow opposite 'for traffic of Harrogate Corporation and Leeds Corporation ... for reservoir works authorised by Harrogate Water Act 1901 and Leeds Corporation Act 1901.' A plan shows (on standard gauge) two 'Harrogate Sidings' and two 'Leeds Sidings', with a 'Joint Road' and runround road located between them, also a 'backshunt' spur towards the Ripon road. The N.E.R. were to operate this link line with their own engines and it has been generally confirmed that this was always so and that the Corporations provided no standard gauge motive power, although one reliable informant differed on this point. The agreement with the Railway Company was cancelled on 31 December 1932 and in the nineteen seventies relatively new walling could be detected where the link line had crossed the road, as could the slightly raised formation of the ensuing curve from the road crossing to the exchange sidings, also that of the 'backshunt.' The three sidings in the goods yard remained until the branch line from Melmerby closed.

Later in 1905 the two Corporations agreed with one another upon the detailed layout and method of operation of the exchange yard and secured the land from the Trustees of the late William Barningham.

The main route on 2ft gauge, Masham to Leighton and Roundhill

The narrow gauge tracks paralleled the standard gauge in the exchange yard but to the north of the standard gauge and there was a transhipment gantry. Towards its westward (outlet) end, the narrow gauge threw off a single track into a locomotive shed on its north side and a coal depot with siding trailed in on its south. The concrete structure of this coal cell could be traced a few years ago. The 'cottage' which survived as a small building in the meadow was close to the locomotive shed.

The line continued westward on a slight embankment – still visible – and soon crossed a by-road and immediately the river Ure; supporting bridge timbers (put in, it is thought, with the aid of a steam pile driver) could until recent years be seen in both banks. The road Masham to Middleham (A6108) was crossed, possibly on the alignment of a present-day overhead line and poles. Next the railway curved south west to cross the Masham–Fearby road and at once the Swinney beck (below height 314ft on the o.s. map). It then proceeded to the north of 'Shaw's farm' and alongside the 'uncoloured' road which by-passes Fearby village on its south side and continued on a near straight westerly course close to the river Burn to reach the spectacular trestle bridge over that river at Leighton Bottom. The bridge carrying the public road to Leighton over the river is immediately north of the trestle's site. Then came Leighton plant yard, already mentioned, with a shed for one 2ft gauge locomotive and, ahead southerly, the original Leighton yard–Fairthorne (Roundhill) line, already described. An account of railway developments undertaken by Leeds will come later.

The Roundhill project for Harrogate: its execution and railway working

The Corporation of Harrogate did not lack for technical advisers. James Mansergh, of Westminster, and Charles Gott were concerned in 1901 with the Water Bill and George F Deacon was retained. T & C Hawksley were engaged for work at Westminster on the Tramroad Bill 1904, while Mr G H Hill (G H Hill & Sons) undertook site inspections and reports at intervals from 1903 onwards. E Wilson Dixon, who had been Harrogate waterworks engineer, continued as such, 1897–1906, with construction at Roundhill occupying much of his time from 1901; from April 1906 until 1911 he retained the post of construction engineer, Roundhill, while relinquishing most of the other responsibilities in the borough. Louis Sykes was resident engineer and John Welton works manager, at Roundhill.

Lands required for Roundhill reservoir were purchased from Lord Masham and Arnagill house was leased from 1901 to 1907 for housing some of the workmen. With agreement, a stone quarry was developed in Arnagill Crag; the face can be seen today and the course of the 2ft gauge incline descending to Roundhill site is clear on the ground.

Roundhill dam is built in the tradition of the Elan and Derwent valleys. It is formed by 4–5 tons individual 'plumbs' of stone set in concrete, the whole faced in handsome worked masonry;

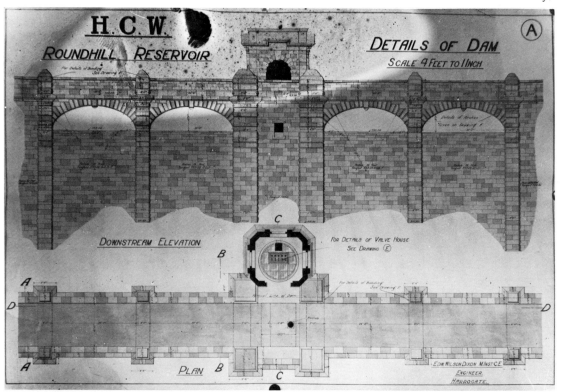

Roundhill dam, from a site drawing of circa 1902 by Edward Wilson Dixon, M.Inst.C.E., waterworks engineer to Harrogate. The central portion of the downstream face of the rockfill dam is shown; the apertures are at future top water level and will take the overflow, as a sheet of water sweeping down this face. In plan, at 'C' the valvetower is depicted.

670ft long and rising 120ft above the bed of the stream, impounding on completion 550 million gallons of water, with top water level 743ft o.d. The works were by direct labour, under E W Dixon. The first sod was cut on 15 July 1903 by Alderman Charles Fortune and completion was achieved in 1911; the dates 1903 and 1911 duly appear on the stonework of the valve tower and a stone in the nearby coping was laid on 13 November 1911 by Captain Archibald Boyd-Carpenter, Mayor of Harrogate.

An aerial ropeway, costing £1920 from John M Henderson of Aberdeen in 1902 and extending across the valley, was employed for much site handling and placing of material. The source of stone was close at hand, with the 2ft gauge incline down from the Crags. The type of construction adopted called for large quantities of cement and during most of the construction period this came from Otto Trechmann & Sons of West Hartlepool; it would constitute the heaviest traffic transhipped in the exchange yard at Masham and hauled up the dale by Harrogate's 2ft gauge locomotives.

The permanent reservoir house, north east of the dam, was early put in hand and carries the date 1903. A village of substantial timber buildings was established on terraces cut into the hillside immediately south east of the dam and above the zig-zags of railway alignment which still stand out. In addition to living quarters, premises included a retail shop and canteen (these being in the charge of George Lamb in the earlier years) and social rooms. The Fairthorne mission of the Navvy Mission Society was set up in 1903, Mr Pickles coming from Scargill reservoir as missioner and Mr Christie succeeding him in 1907, when he was transferred to other works; the mission functioned until Christmas 1910. At first, Mr Pickles was also required to teach the children on weekdays (quite apart from his Sunday school and conducting of services) but a North Riding of Yorkshire County Council School, with its own teacher, was opened in the autumn of 1905. School managers were the chairman of the water committee, the engineer, the missioner and Harry Linton (who represented the workmen). Social events included a Christmas dinner at Corporation expense, from 1904 onwards, and the annual summer sports.

Roundhill dam, constructed 1904–1910, is seen in August 1985 from its water side, the water level falling a little short of the overflow apertures, two each side of the handsome valve tower. View is from near the reservoir house, across the valley to Fairthorne constructional village, to left of the isolated tree. A sighting tower on Arnagill heights is seen; the aqueduct is far below it, in tunnel, penetrated during its making by intriguing German-built steam locomotives.

A distinguished group on the terrace of the permanent Roundhill house, seen newly completed in the early days of the project.

Construction of Roundhill dam is now well advanced, with the valve tower prominent (near right), 2ft gauge track laid onto a gantry (middle left), the overhead ropeway ('blondin') in use, Fairthorne constructional village on the far slope and a locomotive descried (by a keen eye!) – and the sighting tower on the heights.

Taking a telescope to the last scene, in say 1908, the isolated tree is there, much as in 1985, with 'public buildings', and tips, above it, workshops below it (left) and a loco (central); this could be CLARO, 2ft gauge 0-4-2 saddle tank, but with a column added to the safety valve. Climbing half right above the tree, even in 1980s the canteen cellar can be located, fenced around.

'Lord Give Us Our Daily Bread'. One of the 'public buildings' of Fairthorne village is decorated for a religious service, probably a harvest festival. Observe the electric light.

One of the 2ft gauge railway levels comes in (left), with men's accommodation being erected to form the body of Fairthorne village, around 1904.

The village site at its easterly (downstream) end, with railway formations, at an early stage of construction (or at close). The zig-zags to lower levels and, spectacularly, the ascent to Clints quarry (top left of view) are noteworthy.

A midway view up the incline to Clints quarry.

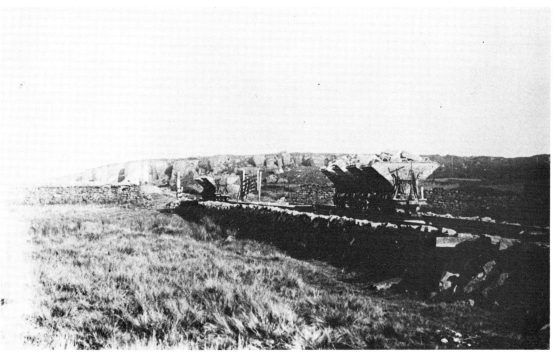

Four loaded steel-bodied tip wagons are coming down 'on the rope' and a 'run' of empties is ascending to Clints quarry.

Here is the incline top, with impressive rockfill blocks for the dam.

Away down again, this is the site of the dam, with the timbered construction trench cutting into the valley side (right, beyond the loco) and a rail mounted steam crane also in use.

A site photograph, titled Fairthorne, shows a locomotive, probably CLARO, seemingly stabled out of use, close to the main workshops at Roundhill village. Locomotives HARROGATE (1902), CLARO (1903) and MASHAM (the largest, 1904) all came new from Leeds steam roller and locomotive builders T Green & Son. Mr Koppel, London agent representing German builders of railway equipment, provided track components and rolling stock – and was probably agent for the special tunnel locomotives MAY and PROGRESS. As the village was so close to the working locations, the daily running of a full workmen's 'Paddy Mail' train was not necessary but, in the early days, a knifeboard-seated vehicle stood nightly at Leighton yard and was run to Roundhill in the mornings, probably by the locomotive which was housed in the shed at the yard. Again, one notes that the accident of May 1911, to be described, involved the late afternoon train from Roundhill, with two passenger vehicles included. A 'Shoppers' Mail' was run on Saturdays, from the site to Masham and back, using both of the knifeboard coaches, which later passed to Leeds Corporation for their use in the dale; note, hereafter, the apposite description of 'jaunting car'. There was also a saloon, for use of engineers, committee and privileged visitors; it had open end balconies and very small wheels and was almost certainly a bogie vehicle.

A charming account of travel to Roundhill appeared in the *Harrogate Advertiser* of 7 October 1905, written by its editor (and reprinted in *Ackrill's Annual*, issue for 1905). It provides both first-hand evidence and atmosphere. The writer travelled in company with W H Breare, editor of *The Herald*, Alderman Fortune (chairman of the water committee) and E W Dixon (the engineer). They left from 'Masham Light Railway station, adjoining the station of the North Eastern Railway, in a comfortable saloon, made at the works of the Corporation, its sides and ends practically all glass; a capital view and a very steady journey, with engine MASHAM, on 2ft gauge, this and the other two locomotives all being built by T Green & Son, Leeds.' The ride continued '... across open fields ... a turnip field, then a pasture, then stubble (with game birds looking on) ... high roads crossed ... woods, ravines ...' The party got out at Leighton bridge and 'heard about an accident on the previous Saturday to one of the Leeds engines, which had gone over broadside a few yards from the junction, on the Leeds line (diverging right to Colsterdale).' The 'Lesser Hotel Majestic'

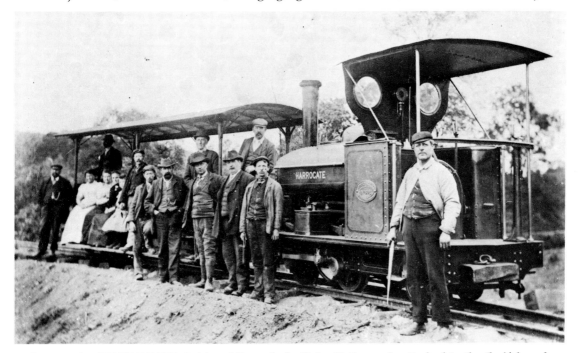

Locomotive HARROGATE, 0-4-2 saddle tank, built by T. Green, is attached to the 'knifeboard carriage'.

was inspected at Leighton bridge – described as a large one storey building, close beside the line, for accommodation of 60 or 70 men of the Harrogate workforce. More passengers joined and the journey continued, reaching 'the village of huts' at Roundhill. Here there was a change to 'a kind of jaunting car, drawn by a little loco, in which the party was whisked to the upper end of Agill to see the settling pond' (of 5–6 million gallons capacity). They subsequently travelled up Arnagill, 'under the bridge of six arches of forty feet span each, carrying the old high road, which had to be diverted, over the railway.' A smaller settling pond was found at the head of Arnagill. There ensues an account of the visit to the dam and village. The Agill and Arnagilll are the two incoming streams at the head of Roundhill reservoir and the trips were to view the intake works on each.

Mr G L Jenkinson, of Streetly in Warwickshire, lived as a youngster, until about 1912, in a house beside the Swinney beck. A family maid was on very friendly terms with the driver of Harrogate's locomotive MASHAM and sometimes, when he was returning with the last trip from Masham sidings, in early evening, he would pick up his girl friend and any members of the Jenkinson family at the crossing east of the Ure; they would enjoy a footplate ride over the river bridge and the Middleham road crossing, being set down at a footpath near the Fearby road.

Reproduced is a view in the exchange sidings – located in the meadow across the road from Masham station – taken on 8 October 1908. On that foggy morning, the North Eastern Railway's goods train, with pipes and materials, hauled by McDonnell 0-6-0 engine No. 208, became out of control on greasy rails approaching Masham. George Walker switched the runaway onto the link line, the crossing keeper stopped traffic and the train charged over the road and piled up in the exchange area. The narrow gauge track will be seen and the transhipment gantry, below which stands the district superintendent from Leeds, seemingly not amused, his assistant deferentially a step behind. In the foreground, one of Mr Atkinson's carts has narrowly escaped disaster. To the left, the photograph omits a narrow gauge locomotive, which its driver is clearly oiling up.

Disaster, 8 October, 1908: **N.E.R. 0-6-0 locomotive No.208, with an incoming goods train, approached Masham out of control and was diverted through that middle siding and over the public road, finishing up derailed near the transhipment gantry and alongside the narrow gauge tracks – in the 'meadow'. To the left, a driver is oiling up his 2ft gauge loco, just off the picture. The N.E.R. superintendent from Leeds is not amused at what he sees. His young assistant stands deferentially silent, likewise the foreman. An 'Atkinson' cart has narrowly escaped.**

The same persons are viewing the scene from the other side, the narrow gauge locomotive's cab is seen above the upturned wagon of Charlesworths, West Riding coalowners.

Rescue is now in hand, close to the gantry.

CLARO with varied merchandise, en route from Masham and nearing Fairthorne. Visible are coal, a stone block (specially imported?), sleepers, bags (of cement?), and long timbers.

Here are the long timbers, in close-up, on a tight curve. This scene is well before 29 May 1911, when disaster occurred to a 'mixed' train, which included timbers in its load.

Above Masham itself, the only church in the valley is that at Healey. Its burial records include the names of three Fairthorne residents whose deaths called for inquests; Charles Mitchell (aged 44 years) killed at the works in June 1904 due to breakage of a wire rope used as a crane sling, James Chadwick (32) who fell down a pit at the works and died in July 1904 and William Spedding (48) whose death occurred in November 1905 after a Saturday night seemingly spent drinking in Healey. In addition, there was a serious accident on the railway in May 1911, recalled by L R Perkins, who was in the dale 1910–14, employed by Arnolds (contractors to Leeds Corporation) on railway work. It resulted in the death of Fred Bartlett (47), who was buried at Healey, and Sam Atkinson, Harrogate's foreman and brother of Arthur Atkinson, lost a leg.

The accident occurred on Monday 29 May 1911, by which time the dam at Roundhill would be essentially complete. The evening train left the site at about 5.40 p.m., bound for Masham, with Harrogate's 0-4-2 Saddle tank locomotive HARROGATE, William Mark West driving. Two bogie wagons heavily loaded with timber were coupled behind the engine and ahead of the two 'mail carts' (which would be the open knifeboard passenger carriages). The driver considered his load to be nearly twenty tons, behind a locomotive quoted as about 7 tons, and before starting he went to George Atkinson (another Atkinson!), foreman fitter, to report the heavy load but Atkinson said that it would be alright provided that the brakes were properly watched. On the way, a gradient of (stated) 1 in 20 down was negotiated successfully. After passing the site of the Leighton dam works the descent was estimated to be 1 in 30 and the brakes were being controlled by West on the engine, by Fred Bartlett at the rear of the first wagon and the front of the second, by Sam Atkinson at the rear of the second wagon and by Albert Campbell, a labourer, on the 'mail coaches', seemingly riding where he could brake the one coach from its rear end and the last coach from its front end. However, approaching the trestle bridge over the stream below Leighton dam site, speed was rising alarmingly and the driver felt the load pushing his engine; William Trevors, a quarryman passenger, said that he saw the engine jerking and skidding and Driver West trying to signal to the brakesmen to apply the vehicle brakes harder. The driver applied steam to try to keep his engine ahead of the train and the bridge was negotiated but on the ensuing curve the first wagon toppled over and brought all or most of the train off the road. Fred Bartlett was trapped and, before his death, said to the driver 'I never released my brake'. Sam Atkinson was also trapped and, on release, was removed to Masham and thence to Leeds Infirmary, where a leg was amputated. Arthur Chamberlain, an inspector on the Leeds works, was a passenger in the rear coach and became alarmed as they crossed the viaduct and jumped off without injury. Other passengers were only shaken. They included Mr S Baldrock, of Ripon, and his brother-in-law, Mr J T Wood, of Rochdale, who were evidently on holiday and had spent an enjoyable day at Roundhill; they afterwards walked to Masham station. Remember Henry Rofe, in 1904, on timber carried by a 'toy railway'!

The Carlesmoor tunnel, passing under the crags, was made by direct labour. The two unusual oil-fired steam locomotives, one located and having its shed at each end of the tunnel, are discussed later, in the tabulated account of the 2ft gauge locomotives. PROGRESS worked into the heading from Roundhill and MAY from the Carlesmoor end. The headings met at 8.0 a.m. on 13 February 1908, the chairman of the waterworks committee and the engineer walking the length of the tunnel on that day.

Reverting to the yard area at Leighton bridge, from the start in 1902 a house was provided there for 'Mr Atkinson', also a shed for his engines; these would be the traction engines provided by Arthur Atkinson but he is generally spoken of as living in Masham – and later he had a Harrogate address – so the house (hut) was more likely occupied by Sam Atkinson, who would be returning home from the works when he was grievously injured in the derailment of 1911. Also in 1902, Mr Cattle was allowed to erect a hut at Leighton, paying Harrogate Corporation £15 per annum and taking Harrogate workmen in preference to Leeds men. This was the 'Lesser Hotel Majestic' of the 1905 account. A minute of December 1908 refers to this hut as 'a common lodging house, the property of Mrs Cattle', who was the occupier and keeper; Masham Urban District Council were critical of its sanitary arrangements.

The saga of the engineer's motor car is amusing. A horse and trap was provided for the use of E W Dixon, on business, but in September 1904 Mr Dixon suggested somewhat cautiously that a second hand motor car might be purchased. Consideration was deferred by the water committee, who evidently gave the matter further thought as in March 1905 they agreed to purchase a car and later in that year decided upon a 24hp Napier car, clearly new. This was acquired and taken into use by Mr Dixon. In the autumn of 1906 he travelled by car to a conference of water engineers in the Derwent valley – where major works were in progress, as described in *Reservoir Railways of Manchester and the Peak*. No doubt the large Napier, a decidedly 'up-market' vehicle, would be much admired. However, in November, it was minuted that, following a resolution of the finance committee, the car was to be sold and the horse and trap retained. A couple of months later, it was noted that only one offer for the car had been received and that was not acceptable (one suspects that the committee had not advertised their car over-assiduously) and the committee decided in the spring of 1907 to keep it for another year. Probably by that time the finance committee had given up the criticism of their colleagues and Mr Dixon would be left to drive in the dales in his horseless carriage.

As the main construction work at Roundhill neared completion, in May 1909, it was decided to carry out cement grouting at the ends of the water face of the dam, in order to ensure tighter sealing into the hillsides, and by 1912 a contract was being negotiated with Harold Arnold & Son, who would do this work; they were then working at Leighton, for Leeds.

From April 1909, surplus plant was advertised and by late 1910 Harrogate wished to sell various huts, plant, engines and dynamos. Sales followed, culminating in a sale at Masham on 3–4 October 1911. In that year Lord Masham was given the option – reserved to him in the negotiations of circa 1902 – to purchase the inclined tramway from Arnagill quarry, but he did not elect to do so. The quarry does not give the impression of having been worked since that time.

The future of the 'Joint Tramroad', namely the main 2ft gauge railway between Leighton yard and Masham exchange yard, was considered in 1911 by Wilson Dixon (Harrogate) and Charles Henzell (Leeds). Leeds Corporation took over responsibility for its future maintenance and in January 1913 Harrogate formally agreed to discontinue their use of the 'Joint Masham Tramroad'. In the spring of 1913, Leeds negotiated with the North Eastern Railway, becoming sole beneficiary of the arrangements for exchange of traffic at Masham.

Carlesmoor tunnel entrance at Fairthorne is seen in construction days. It will accommodate the aqueduct from Roundhill reservoir for Harrogate.

Chapter Three

Leeds in Colsterdale

The Leeds Corporation Water Act, 1901 (17 August)

This Act makes reference to the promotion by Harrogate Corporation, in the same Session, of a Bill to construct Roundhill reservoir on the Pott beck, a tributary of the river Burn.

Works authorised by the Leeds Act (using the numbers in the Act) include:–

1. Colsterdale reservoir on the Burn.
2. Leighton reservoir on the Pott beck, also extending 46 chains up Grimes Gill beck above the confluence, and up the Pott.
4. Aqueduct No. 1: Colsterdale reservoir to Swinsty reservoir.
5. Aqueduct No. 2: from Leighton reservoir to join Aqueduct No. 1.
9. Catchwater (No. 1) from Colsterdale reservoir to Leighton reservoir.
12. Road diversion (No. 5) in the road from Healey to Pott moor.
13. Carlesmoor reservoir, on Carlesmoor beck – extending up that beck and also 42 chains up Stock beck above their confluence.
14. Laverton reservoir, on the river Laver, with its dam immediately north east of the confluence with Carlesmoor beck – extending up the Laver and also up Carlesmoor beck.
15. Aqueduct (No. 3), Carlesmoor reservoir to Aqueduct No. 1.
16. Catchwater (No. 2), commencing in the river Laver at the confluence of North Gill beck and South Gill beck and terminating in Carlesmoor reservoir.

Works Nos. 13 and 14 would have been west of Kirkby Malzeard and Laverton.

The aqueduct for Leeds

Work No. 4 of the 1901 Act involved laying a pipe of 33in internal diameter. For reasons to be explained, it commences at Leighton reservoir. Thence it follows the route of the 2ft gauge railway down the valley to a point almost due south of Fearby, there striking off south easterly, thus avoiding the need to tunnel under Masham moor as was done by Harrogate. There is a break-pressure tank at Kirkby Malzeard. The contracts for laying the steel pipes between Leighton and Kettlesing, via Kirkby Malzeard, went to A Braithwaite & Company, of Leeds, and were executed during 1907–11.

The southerly end of the aqueduct is in Kettlesing tunnel, 2½ miles from Kettlesing to the prominent arm of Swinsty reservoir. The tunnel is of circular section, 6ft diameter, lined with brick. The contractor was John E Kaye (alternatively quoted as J B Kaye), of Huddersfield, but, having started in 1903, Mr Kaye was suing Leeds Corporation by October 1904 and he failed financially in 1905. The waterworks department proceeded by direct labour, 1905–08, with completion in 1908. Various easements for spoil banks were secured from landowners, notably for a shaft, spoil banks *and tramway* on lands of Beck farm at Norwood; that is, north east of the arm of Swinsty reservoir. This activity was during 1904, and probably the ensuing years.

It was proposed to acquire two traction engines and trailer trucks, to carry bricks to the tunnel works, but the main waterworks committee speedily decided (9 September 1904) against traction engines and trucks, probably having painful memories of the problems when such equipment was tried on haulage to Swinsty reservoir. Instead, S Latham carried bricks from Starbeck station, with the alternative of using Darley station on the Pateley Bridge line. Hauling gear for incline work was supplied (1906) by John Fowler & Company Limited, of Leeds, and this would involve steam plant.

Colsterdale reservoir project: a chronology

  Authorised by their Act of 1901, Leeds resolved that Colsterdale reservoir in the valley of the Burn, with an earth embankment and capacity of 1852 million gallons, should be the first reservoir constructed. The plans for this work greatly influenced the development of Leeds Corporation railways and the siting of their huge construction village – of which more anon. Significant events of 1904–06 are presented as a chronology:–

14 September 1904:	five tenders received and three are to be considered, namely – George Bell (but he withdrew – and shortly took on aqueduct construction for the Derwent Valley Water Board, Chatsworth) Robert McAlpine & Sons H Arnold & Son
24 October 1904:	committee proposed provisional acceptance of the tender from McAlpines, £296,863.18.3d
28 October 1904:	*Building News* reported letting to McAlpines, at this price.
9 November 1904:	the Council referred the tender back.
9 December 1904:	committee decided to seek report from Charles Hawksley, Westminster, on the plans and specifications for Colsterdale.
23 January 1905:	committee proposed to ask McAlpines and Arnolds to reconsider their tenders but then decided to take an opinion from James Watson, the notable waterworks engineer of Bradford; at his suggestion, all five tenders were laid before him.
27 January 1905:	*Building News* reported that, on 23 January, the Council had decided to build the reservoir themselves (a misunderstanding?).
30 March 1905:	Mr Watson has recommended McAlpines, at their quoted price, and this recommendation is to be accepted.
5 April 1905:	the Council agreed to appoint Charles George Henzell, M.I.C.E., as their waterworks engineer, salary £1,000 p.a. and agreed progression to £1,500 (mysteriously, they rescinded the appointment at 9 November 1905, but in fact Mr Henzell occupied the post with distinction from April 1905 until 31 December 1924).
(5?) April 1905:	the contract was let to McAlpines.
7 April 1905:	*Building News* records this for the second time!
concurrently:	Mr Henzell commenced his own investigation, presumably of the site rather than contractors: 'work slowed, little done'.
9 June 1905:	serious slips reported in the side of the valley; the consultant Henry Rofe is to be asked to visit Colsterdale.
13 September 1905:	Mr Rofe recommended acquiring more land and undertaking more investigation of strata, before any work is done.
9 November 1905:	the contract with McAlpines is rescinded.
20 April 1906:	Mr Rofe is to consult with Dr Boyd Dawkins (distinguished geologist) concerning the geological information obtained before the Bill went to Parliament.
27 August 1906:	on the recommendation of C G Henzell and H Rofe, the committee resolved to apply to Parliament to abandon the construction of Colsterdale reservoir and to construct a reservoir on the Burn, with dam 825 chains south east of Body Close House (farm) and to alter aqueduct No. 1 and extend catchwater No. 1 to Spruce gill. (This represents a resiting of Leighton reservoir and tapping the waters of Spruce gill, in Colsterdale, direct to Leighton reservoir.)
5 October 1906:	the Council resolved to proceed with Leighton, as recommended by Henzell and Rofe.

N.B: The waterworks committee's annual report to 31 March 1907 gives a decidedly misleading account of the year's decisions, so is not quoted.

Carlesmoor, Laverton – and Colsterdale again

During the early years of the twentieth century, Leeds acquired from Lord Ripon (the Marquis of Ripon) estates of about 2300 acres, including control of forty-one tenancies in the Laver valley. However, the authorised reservoirs at Carlesmoor and Laverton were not put in hand.

In 1952, the Carlesmoor project was revived, in conjunction with a 'New Colsterdale' reservoir, the latter with its dam on a different site from that intended in 1901–06. Each reservoir would have its own pipeline to the break-pressure tank at Kirkby Malzeard, where the water would be brought to a common head, along with that from Leighton. Three pipelines would run from the tank to Kettlesing tunnel, to convey all the impounded waters to Swinsty reservoir. These works have not, up to the present, been undertaken.

Leeds at Leighton: debate, 1908

On 17 January 1908, the waterworks committee turned down a tender submitted (with qualifications) by Mr Scott (meaning John Scott of Darlington?) and were left with two competing contractors for constructing Leighton reservoir –

Morrison & Mason (of Glasgow) – £432,197.7.0d
H Arnold & Son (of Leeds – and Doncaster) – £437,182.0.0d

The tenders were referred to Charles Hawksley (Westminster) and James Watson (Bradford) and both engineers preferred Morrison & Mason, on grounds of greater relevant experience. This was seemingly not the answer desired so reference was made to Ernest J Mansergh (Westminster) and George H Hill (of G H Hill & Sons, Manchester). Mansergh favoured Arnolds but Hill, whose firm had known them for twenty years on major schemes involving deep trenches, recommended Morrison & Mason. Charles Henzell, the Corporation's own engineer, visited Craigmaddie (bank ¾ mile long and trench of great depth, over 200ft), consulting Glasgow water department and Watson, also viewing current works of Arnolds at Carlisle, Skipton and Ilkley. He recommended M & M. After an interregnum, not minuted, the committee recommended Arnolds. The full Council considered the reports, in which four technical advisers, including their own engineer, had favoured Morrison & Mason. On 1 July 1908, they accepted the tender of H Arnold & Son – of Leeds.

Leeds at Leighton: contract works, 1908–1915

With all speed, on 14 July 1908, the first sod was cut at Leighton, in the presence of the Council, and Arnolds made a prompt and businesslike start; there was never complaint of their work. By the spring of 1909, they had acquired a 'Blondin', a 3 tons capacity Henderson cableway 1875 ft long, with two 80 ft steel masts, from the Conisborough viaduct works of the Dearne Valley Railway and erected it across the valley – where, already, the main trench was excavated to depths between 6ft and 90ft. By March 1911, the full length of the trench had been excavated, 186ft deep at its maximum, and the engineers had decided that it would be prudent to construct a spur trench, at right angles to the main trench for 50ft westwards in the southern valley side – with the possibility that further work might be required, if leakage occurred through this side of the valley. Messrs Henzell, Rofe and Watson also decided (April 1911) to enclose unreliable clay beneath the main trench within substantial concrete walls. The routine filling of the trench with concrete had begun in November 1909 and was nearly complete by March 1912. Placing of puddle clay (atop the concrete) began in April 1911 and formation of the earthfill embankment in 1911–12.

At 31 March 1914, nearly half the 'fill' had been placed in the embankment, which was up to 553ft o.d. (designed top of bank to be 612ft o.d.). The puddle clay filling was about half done. Diversion of the public road had been completed and traffic was using it. Work went on day and night during May–November 1912 and again from 16 March 1914. The contractors' workforce, mostly averaging around 450 in the earlier years, reached 500 in August 1914 but the job was immediately affected by the war – more quickly than at most comparable sites – and in winter

1914–15 numbers were around 180, still working night and day on embankment, puddling and building the bywash. The entire works closed down on 1 April 1915, suspension being agreed between the Leeds Corporation and Arnolds; during 1915–16, all the contractors' men and much plant were transferred away. Arnolds were fortunate to move directly to work upon a huge military camp near Ripon and other wartime works, including the building of the Great Northern Railway's High Dyke branch line, near Grantham, to develop new ironstone quarries.

The stone quarry developed by Arnolds for Leighton was at Arnagill, where a vast amphitheatre in the crags, east of Harrogate's quarry face, is today evidence of work for and by Leeds. An inclined railway (on 3ft gauge) was put in by Arnolds from this stone quarry to the vicinity of the dam site, southern end, and the course can be seen, and traversed with a scramble.

The quarry was the scene of a spectacular and tragic accident, which occurred first thing on the morning of 3 May 1911, following a particularly wet night. Arnolds' four-coupled saddle tank locomotive NIDD was engaged in tipping duties and being driven up a track close above a part of the quarry face to fetch the wagons (one recollection was that wagons were attached); it became derailed and toppled over the edge of the quarry, falling some thirty feet. Harry Adams, rope runner, jumped off the engine in time but the unfortunate driver failed to escape and was killed instantly when the NIDD fell on him. He was James Barker, of Breary Banks, and after an inquest was buried in Healey churchyard on Saturday 6 May. It is on record that he was known as 'Brimy' or 'Brum' Barker – presumably from having lived or worked in Birmingham. He was a very popular man and a keen photographer of local scenes. He left a wife and nine children. Although badly damaged, NIDD was eventually repaired and resumed work, but not in the quarry. Mr Perkins later worked on NIDD in the bottom of the valley, presumably in conjunction with the excavation and deepening of the reservoir site.

The clay for puddling was secured from fields north west of the dam site and beyond the (diverted) public road. Earthfill came from the same general area, towards Grimes gill, although it may be that in the pre-1915 days much of it was out of the valley bottom.

The contractor's offices, workshops and plant yard were established level with the new road and the top of the eventual dam, where the permanent waterworks houses have been built. Arnolds' locomotive shed, in timber with an iron roof, had two roads, accommodating 3ft gauge locomotives, and was on just about the site where the Corporation bungalows now stand. There was exchange between 2ft and 3ft gauge in this area, but no mixed gauge layout. The main reservoir house was complete by March 1910 and available for the Corporation's resident engineer. Inlet works on Spruce gill, in upper Colsterdale – involving a masonry dam – were constructed in 1911–12 and by 1914 the catchwater to bring the gill's waters to Leighton was progressing, notwithstanding a frustrating landslip.

Leeds at Leighton: direct labour, 1921–1926

Renewed activity was first prompted by a landslip in May 1920, on the north slope of the valley and about 300 yards upstream of the partly formed embankment. Arnolds, not surprisingly, accepted no responsibility. Eventually, around mid-1921, the Corporation built a large concrete toe wall, with suitable drainage. When planning the work, Charles Henzell visited Richborough in Kent to purchase a locomotive and six steel wagons; these items would be from War Department surplus stock and it would be a petrol locomotive for 2ft gauge.

In October 1921, influenced by the scale of unemployment in Leeds and district, the City Council decided to terminate the long-suspended contract with Arnolds and complete Leighton reservoir by direct labour under Mr Henzell. Some 250 men were employed through the winter 1921–22, over 150 being previously unemployed and from Leeds; the work was mainly hauling fill to the embankment by way of the site railway and placing it; likewise hauling and putting in puddle clay. By the end of the winter, Arnagill quarry, below Clints Crags, was reopened and it provided stone for various purposes, including pitching to protect the water face of the dam. There had been a supplementary Leeds Corporation Act, 1913, and now an Order was sought from the Ministry of Health under the Special Acts (Extension of Time) Act, 1915, authorising completion.

In addition to light railway equipment, with mainly petrol locomotives, two steam navvies were secured, the second one (August 1922) being a new Ruston machine, with caterpillar tractor, at £1905; also locomotive type and derrick steam cranes.

Work proceeded steadily until, in September 1924, with the embankment only a few feet short of full height, heavy rainfall caused movement of the inside slope in an area done by direct labour, with bulging and dislodging of pitching stonework. Extra work followed; dry, stony material was added to the rubble toe of the bank and the slope above it was regraded to average 5 to 1, previously being 3½ to 1. This work and completion of the embankment continued through to about March 1926, but with a reduced workforce. A major sale of plant and materials took place on 13–15 July 1926.

Leeds at Leighton: sequel, 1927–1941

The reservoir was filled in winter 1926–27, right up to the level of the waste weir (overflow), which at 615ft o.d. is a few feet above the intended (1915) height of the embankment, implying some subsequent modification. Above 572ft o.d., water escaped through bad rock at the south end of the embankment, but clear of the embankment itself – much as suspected (in 1910) might eventually occur. Investigation and 400 yards of cementation along the south shore were completed by July 1929, along with a 'bypass pipeline' on this shore. Owing to drought, Leeds had only thirty-one days' supply in its reservoirs on 29 September 1929, when water was taken for the first time from Leighton, through the aqueduct to Swinsty and so indirectly to Leeds. This continued until 31 October. Leighton was then allowed to fill and overflowed on 29 December, with the leakage reduced by 80 per cent. More cementation was done and by the end of 1931, 15000 tons of cement had been used in the work and the strengthened shore extended for approximately 1000 yards along the reservoir's south side. Significantly, the Corporation's 'main line' railway from Masham had been maintained throughout. And there was yet more cementation in 1936–41. Capacity of Leighton reservoir is some 1050 million gallons at top water level of 615ft o.d.

Leeds at Leighton: personalities

Consultants of the pre-1915 era have been mentioned. James Watson (Bradford) died on 29 March 1919. Charles Henzell was lost to Leeds water through illness (January 1924) and ensuing resignation (December 1924). Their favoured consultant in the 'twenties was J K Swales (Bolton Corporation), who had formerly been on their staff. He in turn called H P Hill (Manchester) into consultation (1924). E J Silcock was consultant in 1927, when the south shore came to be strengthened.

J K Swales had been the Corporation's first resident engineer at Leighton (November 1907), then A G Beaumont (January 1911, with occupation of the permanent house) and S T A Neil (October 1913). From May 1919, S A Smith was resident engineer, Leighton, until April 1926. Construction was then essentially complete and the first resident reservoir keeper was appointed, R Metcalfe.

After the incapacity and consequent resignation of C G Henzell as waterworks engineer to the city, protracted indecision followed and it was left to H Shortreed, formerly chief clerk, to take charge of the department. He became manager from 1 April 1927, with W F Smith as engineer and assistant manager.

The village at Breary Banks

In March 1903, the city engineer of Leeds reported an outbreak of smallpox in a 'common lodging house' at Masham and this would point to the need for proper accommodation for the workforce – visualised by Leeds waterworks committee in 1903–4 as likely to attain at least 700, plus families. So the village of Breary Banks was created. It has come to be part of the folklore of Masham and Colsterdale, indeed of Leeds itself, and deserves an account in its own right.

The site selected was well up the southern slope of Colsterdale proper, as indicated on our map. Water supply was provided, being pumped by a water wheel (powered by the river) from a spring in the valley to a small reservoir 300ft higher. Proper drainage and also sewage treatment

LEEDS No.1, which will feature again, hauling timbers.

LEEDS No.1 is delivering 'Quaker oats', presumably at Breary Banks. I debate whether this is in waterworks construction times, or during military occupation. The many helpers are in mufti, smart attire, and of remarkably varied ages.

beds were installed. Electric lighting was put in from the start; the generating plant (with boiler, steam turbine and electric generator) was moved a little northward around 1908 to the power house (of which foundations survive) beside the river near Gollinglith, shown on our map. Trucks (2ft gauge) of coal were lowered down an inclined track, partly on now-vanished timber staging, from near the Colsterdale dead end on the Leeds railway. From near the same dead end, a very steep adhesion-worked branch line trailed back to deliver coals and provisions to the village.

By spring 1904, huts had been built for 400 men and others were being erected. The streets were titled First, Second, Third, Fourth, Fifth and Sixth Avenues, complete with nameplates. In 1908–09, 24 additional huts were built, enlarging the village; in general, each living hut accommodated 16 navvies, with sleeping and living quarters, bath and w.c., also accommodation for the caretaker and family. A Corporation photograph (date uncertain) shows some fifty wooden buildings, including the 'public buildings' of the village.

A reading and recreation room, with billiard table, was provided and placed under the care of the missioner, as was the mission room, equipped – it is believed – with an 'American organ'. The mission room was opened by Mrs Grimston, wife of the Hon. R Grimston, superintendent of the Navvy Mission Society. The first missioner was Walter Barbour (or Barlow), whose services were shortly taken over by the Corporation from the Navvy Mission Society. When he resigned in 1911, Myles Miller was appointed navvy missioner in Colsterdale, at £78 per annum, with house, coals and light provided. The missioner was permitted to sell coffee and soft drinks in the recreation room. A licenced canteen was also established and soon (1905) this was placed under the management of the Peoples' Refreshment House Association Ltd, with T Manning in charge.

The mission building, seating 300 people, seems to have doubled up in daytime as the village school, 'Masham Waterworks School', when this was set up in 1905. Its governors represented the education committee of the North Riding of Yorkshire County Council, the waterworks committee of Leeds Corporation, also the Healey Parish Council. From autumn 1909, Breary Banks school excluded children under five years; evidently there was by then pressure on the accommodation. About this time, the recreation room was enlarged, so this may have helped the school too. There was a house for the schoolmaster, but it is not on record what staff he had.

There was a site hospital and a doctor in private practice attended three days each week and also when required urgently.

Two general stores were let to tradesmen from Masham during the years of peak activity at Breary Banks. The village had access by narrow gauge railway and one may judge that the community enjoyed an active and usually pleasant life. Sometimes, at about 750ft up in the dales, the hard winters took their toll. For example, in January 1912, the chairman and deputy chairman of Leeds waterworks committee were considering opening a soup kitchen, as distress had resulted from the bad weather. It would be a case of no work, no pay.

A permanent Wesleyan chapel was built near Breary Banks camp. Lord Masham presented the site and some old buildings adjoining. The foundation stone was laid on Saturday 19 August 1911 by Harry Middlebrook, of Morley. He was deputising for his father, the Lord Mayor of Leeds, who had intended to perform the ceremony but was prevented by the grave labour unrest of the period. The Reverend T Rowson was the presiding minister. A special train for participants was run from Masham to Breary Banks and back – without charge – by the kindness of Arthur Atkinson. This circumstance supports the understanding that Mr Atkinson was agent for the operation of the 2ft gauge railway at the period. The tiny 'Wesleyan Chapel 1911' survives into 1991, but seemingly inactive.

Near the chapel and level crossing on the road to Breary Banks, 'The Bungalow' was built – and still stands, with a closely adjoining new house in course of erection, 1990–91. It was available to visiting engineers and the waterworks committee for meals, also for overnight stays. Council members not on the committee paid five shillings per day for board. There was (and is) a permanent building across the valley from Breary Banks. This was 'The White House' (with red roof) which was intended for the keeper of the planned Colsterdale reservoir but was occupied by Mr Arnold, the contractor for Leighton; it is known nowadays as 'Pasture House'.

Military days and after

Is the load a mix of ammunition and beer?

LEEDS No.1 now lacks its lettering but its driver has been joined by a distinguished commanding officer (and his lady), and a substantial military company – thought to be in Masham exchange yard, bound for the camp at Breary Banks.

Breary Banks: the military connection

As early as September 1914 land at Breary Banks, below the road, was made available to the War Office for an army camp, which was promptly occupied by 'The Leeds Pals'. They were the 15th Battalion (1st Leeds), West Yorkshire Regiment, raised by Lord Brotherton.

Arthur Pearson, then already enlisted in the 'Pals', has recalled that they travelled from Leeds to Masham in two special trains, and marched from the station to Breary Banks, on Friday 25 September 1914. They occupied part of the hutted reservoir village, with overflow accommodation under canvas, the officers living in 'The Bungalow'. Over one thousand men were in training here in Colsterdale during the winter 1914–15. Huts were erected below the road and a rifle range was created. The Battalion left Colsterdale on 25 May 1915, bound in that year for Egypt, going thence to France early in 1916. Disaster ensued in the Battle of the Somme, 1 July 1916, when the Battalion was tragically depleted, losing over five hundred officers and men in one day. Alderman Willey, chairman of Leeds waterworks committee for many years, lost his son and Captain Stanley Neil – still nominally resident engineer at Leighton and occupant of the reservoir house – was killed in the same calamity.

As the constructional workforce ran down in 1914–15, and departed, every significant building of the waterworks village was leased to the War Office. In the year to 31 March 1916, reserves of the 15th (Leeds), 19th (Bradford) and 20th Battalions of the West Yorkshires had sojourned at Breary Banks and been succeeded there by the 15th Reserve Battalion of the York and Lancaster Regiment. During part of 1916, a Battalion of 'transport workers' were stationed at the camp but from January 1917 it was used for housing German officer prisoners of war, under War Office control but with Leeds Corporation supplying electricity and running the canteen – and using the railway for supplies. The War Office later manned the power house and added engine-driven generating plant. It was not until October 1919 that the last prisoners departed from the site. Leeds regained nominal possession from 28 November 1919, fully from early 1920, and put in hand during 1920–21 reinstatement of the village for their own prospective needs.

Breary Banks: after 'the occupation'

During 1921–22, the waterworks village at Breary Banks gradually came back to life, with the provision stores let to Mr Watkinson, the canteen again under P.R.H.A. Ltd management and the Industrial Christian Fellowship (formerly the Navvy Mission Society) appointing a resident navvy missioner from February 1922. The school, closed in 1915, was brought into use, on the pre-war terms, from September 1922.

By March 1923, 49 huts were in occupation and – as earlier noted – the workforce reached a peak in 1922–24, followed by rapid decline in 1924–27. A cinema (by March 1923) and a wireless set in the recreation room (by March 1924) were new refinements. Soon the maximum activity was over and the canteen closed at the end of June 1926, by which time sale and removal of buildings was taking place. Names, probably from this era, recalled by Eric Ramsden in *Dalesman* November 1974 included his father as schoolmaster, Wilson as village superintendent, Storey the policeman and Gore the canteen manager, also Thomas Legge the locomotive driver.

Today, the war memorial of 1935 stands as a reminder of the lively navvies' village of Arnolds' day, the hopeful recruits of 1914–15 (and ensuing tragedy), the German era and the brief peak of life and activity in the nineteen-twenties. The village site was on the slopes behind the memorial and from here one may look across the valley to 'The White House', visualise Colsterdale reservoir that never was, and trace on the ground the railway layout which was part of Breary Banks.

Railways for Leeds (and contractors): Masham to Colsterdale and Leighton

The new 2ft gauge line of 1905–07, constructed by Leeds Corporation, initially to give access to the intended Colsterdale dam site and the village at Breary Banks, branched just west of the trestle, near Leighton bridge and yard. It ran north westward for a mile, crossing first the road to Breary Banks village and then a substantial viaduct (pier bases still visible) to reach its dead end by the Spruce Gill beck in Colsterdale. This was where the winch-operated branch dropped away rightwards to the Colsterdale road near Gollinglith farm – conveying power house coal and

The memorial, unveiled in 1935, at Breary Banks camp site, is seen in 1985. It acknowledges the sojourn here, in 1914–1915, of the 15th Battalion, West Yorkshire Regiment (Leeds Pals), so many of whom lost their lives on the Somme on 1 July 1916.

From the same spot, we now look south east across the valley of Spruce Gill and the River Burn – where 'Colsterdale reservoir' was intended to figure. On the far side is 'the white house', onetime residence of Harold Arnold, whose firm set to work on Leighton reservoir. Edward (Teddy) Mills (see Preface) is conducting our travels. Michael Davies and (right) Arther Chambers examine a relevant map sheet. During 1904–1932, Leeds Corporation's 2ft gauge Colsterdale branch line came nearly to the fence beside which the author's Sunbeam-Talbot car stands.

facilitating collection of some road deliveries. There was also a short horse-operated section of line which brought outcrop stone over the road at Gollinglith to the vicinity of the incline foot. In later times there was a short-lived line up Colsterdale, beyond Gollinglith, powered by a petrol locomotive and used for recovering pipes.

When work had to be concentrated upon Leighton reservoir in preference to Colsterdale, the railway route was extended, with a reversal of direction, from a point a little short of the Colsterdale dead end. The extension route crossed the village road just below the chapel (standing) and proceeded along the hillside, its course almost marked by the present day fenced conduit carrying Spruce Gill (beck), to negotiate reverse curves and cross the Leighton road at a point identified by two farmhouses, thence to the north west upper corner of the future dam, in the area where administration, site stores, workshops and plant yard were established.

This was the end of the 2ft gauge 'high level' route, as Arnolds elected to bring track, rolling stock and many steam locomotives (of which particulars follow) *built to the 3ft gauge* – favoured by waterworks builders. Arnolds progressively developed an extensive 3ft gauge system within a fairly compact area; lines served diggers in the reservoir bed, others brought earthfill and clay from above the road on the northern shore, and the incline descended from Arnagill quarry, Clints Craggs. The foot of this incline effectively converged on the Harrogate 2ft gauge route from Roundhill (a gate in the stone wall is opposite the convergence) but the complication of two gauges in this vicinity was eliminated by the virtual cessation of Harrogate traffic around 1910. One should add that Arnolds made some local use of 2ft gauge, with two steam locomotives, on a tip.

Leeds decided in September 1904 that they would require a 2ft gauge steam locomotive, six wagons and one carriage, and orders were soon placed. The locomotive was (for its gauge) a powerful 0-6-2 Side tank engine, of neat appearance, delivered by Hunslet Engine Company on 24 January 1905 at the price of £1175, carrying the name LEEDS NO. 1. Trucks, at £7.7.0d each, came from Robert Hudson and a passenger carriage for the committee cost £70. Hudson also provided rails but by 1907 second hand steel rails for the Leighton extension were supplied by Marple & Gillott.

Although the main railway route, constructed on the initiative and under the arrangements of Harrogate Corporation, was nominally of 2ft gauge, there is evidence that this rail gauge was not strictly adhered to. A Harrogate minute of 12 December 1904 notes that the gauge of the railway was discussed between the Town Clerk of Harrogate and the Town Clerk of Leeds; further, that a Harrogate sub-committee saw the Town Clerk of Leeds and agreed to meet the expense of altering the Leeds locomotive and their rolling stock already built 'to fit the gauge of the railway as laid down'. Incidentally, the terms for the use of the railway ('tramway') were formally agreed between the two authorities in course of the next few days. The makers' specification for LEEDS NO. 1 was dated 17 September 1904 and shows 'Gauge of Railway 2 feet 0 inches.' The makers' order book (a roughly contemporary entry) shows '2'-0"' However, their engine book (register of locomotives built) records '1'-11⅝"' (and this manuscript entry may well have been inserted over an erasure of '2'-0"'). A printed sheet for publicity and catalogue purposes, headed by a photograph of Hunslet 865, painted in shop grey, states: 'Gauge of Railway 1ft. 11⅝ in.' (which is closer to 60cm than is 2ft). It is careful not to specify whose railway this was.

The three locomotives built by T Green & Son for Harrogate, and delivered between June 1902 and September 1904, seem to have run satisfactorily in service but the larger and heavier 0-6-2 Tank LEEDS NO. 1 was soon in trouble. On 27 March 1905, it was agreed that Harrogate's engineer and the resident engineer for Leeds would inspect the track together, 'in view of the difficulty in keeping the Leeds locomotive on the rails.' The sequel was an order of 27 April 1905 from Leeds to Hunslet Engine Company to modify the trailing pony truck of LEEDS NO. 1, in order to allow greater freedom of movement. The pony truck was altered from a design with outside frames and bearings to one with inside frames and bearings. This was neatly achieved by machining new bearing journals on the axle inside the wheels and removing the outer ends of the axle, which had provided the outside journals. The right hand frame of the pony truck was transferred from a position outside the right wheel to inside the left wheel, and vice versa. The existing hornblocks, axleboxes and spring gear were used.

LEEDS NO. 1 was one of many 0-6-2 and 2-6-2 Tank engines for narrow gauge railways built by the Hunslet Engine Company, with fairly minor variations. Its cylinders, wheels, motion and brake gear were identical with those fitted to Hunslet's 2-6-2 Side tanks first built in 1898 for the Sierra Leone Government Railways 2ft 6in gauge (cf. S.L.R. No. 85, of 1954, now on the Welshpool & Llanfair Light Railway, in Wales; No. 85 is very similar to earlier Sierra Leone Hunslets but has ¾in greater cylinder diameter, like LEEDS NO. 1). The boiler of the Leeds locomotive was slightly larger than the 1898 design and the Leeds boiler drawings were used for RUSSELL of 1906, built for the North Wales Narrow Gauge Railway and happily existing today.

The only other 'main line' steam locomotive known to have been employed by Leeds was Harrogate 0-6-2 Tank MASHAM, believed purchased to help LEEDS NO. 1 in the early period of Leighton works, but disposed of from the area in 1912.

It is minuted at 21 August 1908, concurrent with sale of surplus plant from Colsterdale proper to Arnolds, that 'a locomotive and wagons were sold for £650 to Arthur Atkinson of Masham.' If the locomotive was LEEDS NO. 1 the price is surprisingly low but it is also significant that from 1909 to at least 1920, including the war years, all makers' spares for LEEDS NO. 1 were ordered by A Atkinson. It is known that this locomotive, originally housed in a shed at Breary Banks, moved under Atkinson's influence to its better known engine shed at Masham exchange sidings. The indications, from minutes and memories, are that Arthur Atkinson worked the 2ft 'main line' as agent, for Leeds Corporation. Arthur Atkinson has been recalled living in a house near the bend in the road, between Masham station and the Ure bridge, on the way to the village and dale. His address here in 1909–16 was 'The Grotto', Masham, and by June 1916 it changed to Station Parade, Harrogate. 'The Grotto' survives as 'The Greens'.

A pleasant sidelight on working of the railway appears in the Institution of Water Engineers' Journal, 1910, reporting the Institution's Yorkshire meeting of that year, no doubt a summer gathering for members and ladies and believed to be based on York. On Friday of the meetings, a special train was run to Masham, where Charles Henzell and representatives of H Arnold & Sons received the party for an afternoon visit. Travel was by the light railway to Leighton site, followed by tea at 'The Bungalow' with Councillor Willey, chairman of the committee, as host.

During the military era in Colsterdale, locomotive LEEDS NO. 1 and its driver maintained a daily service with stores for Breary Banks camp. Recollection of the early wartime period is that troops only used the railway when going on leave, joining the narrow gauge train at the road crossing near the chapel and travelling in wagons devoid of seats to the exchange yard near Masham station. The general responsibility for the railway rested at this period with the military authorities and, by 1917–18 and through to 1920, considerable repair of the track and bridges was called for; it was undertaken by the War Office, to the satisfaction of the Corporation, who shared the cost. The railway was handed back around January 1920.

On resuming work at Leighton, the Corporation appear to have taken over Arnolds' 3ft gauge tracks in the quarry and on the incline down from it; they employed two 3ft gauge steam locomotives on quarry duties. It is minuted (9 October 1922) 'that the engineer is to purchase a secondhand steam locomotive for Leighton from a list submitted to him, subject to inspection; also to visit Brimsdown and Newport (Mon) to inspect steam locomotives'. The outcome of these negotiations is likely to have been the acquisition of two wartime forestry locomotives, built by Kerr Stuart of Stoke as Nos 3083 and 3084 in their books, both being 0-6-0 Side tank engines with outside cylinders 8½in x 11in. A one time Arnold locomotive, the NIDD, also worked for the Corporation on 3ft gauge.

For the rest, Leeds Corporation laid light 2ft gauge tracks around the site area, in place of Arnolds' 3ft – which had been removed some years before – and acquired petrol locomotives. References have been traced to eleven such purchases (or intended purchases) between May 1921 and November 1924. Sources included Richborough, Ashford, Newcastle, Sunderland and Marske, implying government surplus machines, some overhauled (e.g. by Kent Construction & Engineering Company, of Ashford, who were in this business). There were in total considerably more than eleven, as at 31 March 1923 and again at 31 March 1924, '23 locos and engines' were at work, plus two steam navvies. By 31 March 1925, '17 engines' were reported at work on the embankment and in the quarry, with '7 engines' at 31 March 1926. 2 ft gauge steel trucks came from government sources and from J & F Howard, of Bedford, and from Robert Hudson Ltd. Track materials were from T W Ward Ltd., and elsewhere.

Spares were ordered for four internal combustion locomotives as late as July 1926 but the main sale of plant was held in that month and included '115 2ft and 3ft side tip wagons, and locomotives'.

Changing times are evidenced by settlement of Mr J A Chapman's claim for £5 for damage to a motor car by a locomotive on the light railway (10 July 1922) and settlement on 13 July 1925 at £134.3.0d of a claim by J F Latimer for damages and personal injuries due to collision of his motor car with a light engine of the committee at the level crossing near Masham, on 4 March 1925.

It is interesting that in May 1922 the waterworks committee 'approved the purchase from Mr A Atkinson of the rolling stock, plant and buildings used in connection with the light railway between Masham station and the works, for £658.17.6d.' Note that Atkinson ordered spares for the main line steam locomotive, LEEDS NO. 1, until at least 1920.

Mr J W Armstrong explored the lines as then existing on 6 June 1926, shortly before the sale of July that year. At Masham exchange area were found:

3ft gauge: locomotive NIDD 0-4-0 Saddle tank, noted as W G Bagnall 1658, also unnamed loco 0-6-0 Tank by Kerr Stuart 3083 of 1917 (and one may note that only one KS loco was offered for sale in July 1926, presumably this one).
2ft gauge (presumed): two 4 wheel internal combustion locos, Simplex type, Nos 421 and 464. (Both would be 40hp; believed ex-W.D.L.R. 2142 and 2185, respectively)
2ft gauge: LEEDS NO. 1 0-6-2 Tank loco by Hunslet Engine Company 865 of 1904.

The locomotive LEEDS NO. 1 had an overhaul after the war, in 1919, and when the main post-war work came to an end it retired to its shed at Masham, cared for, albeit informally, by its long-time driver Tom Legge; he was an old hand in public works, with experience of the Manchester Ship Canal and other contracts.

Some two years after Mr Armstrong's visit, Mr Humphrey Household called at Masham yard (exchange sidings) late in March 1928 and found various wagons for possible disposal, while LEEDS NO. 1 was well sheeted. In that summer, Mr Household paid another visit, finding LEEDS NO. 1 vanished (its disposal is mentioned later). He also noted two Simplex tractors on the line there, quoting one as 40hp and the other as 20hp, the smaller of these actually being at work; they appeared to be retained to shift wagons on the 2ft gauge.

In early summer 1926, it was decided to maintain the light railway until Leighton reservoir had been tested – and remember that serious leakage through its southern shore was found on filling in winter 1926–27.

Easements for the main route of the light railway were extended from time to time by landowners, for example at 9 August 1926 (for twelve months, without charge, by Lady Cunliffe-Lister), at 12 September 1927 (until 31 December 1929, by Swinton Park Settled Estates).

In February 1929, it was agreed with Harrogate Corporation to transport pipes on the light railway, from Masham sidings to Roundhill reservoir; clearly, these loads would complete their journey by road from Leighton dam to Roundhill.

Finally, during the year 1 April 1932 to 31 March 1933, the light railway between Masham sidings and Leighton reservoir, noted as over six miles, was lifted, and restoration of the land on its route was effected by Swinton Park Settled Estates, at a cost of £1600 to Leeds Corporation. The sidings in the exchange yard at Masham were vacated during the year and the tracks here too were lifted.

It is not clear what locomotives provided power for the limited use of the light railway after summer 1926 and eventually during the lifting operations of 1932–33.

Harrogate Corporation's 2ft gauge HARROGATE (T Green, 301 of 1902)

Harrogate Corporation's 2ft gauge CLARO (T Green, 312 of 1903)

Chapter Four

Locomotives in Colsterdale

Locomotives (steam), 2ft gauge, employed on lines above Masham, period 1902–26, or later

Most of the engines for the narrower 2ft gauge (as distinct from those on 3ft gauge) started life in the dales above Masham as property of Harrogate Corporation but tended to pass to Arthur Atkinson, Harold Arnold & Son or Leeds Corporation; it is therefore convenient to include them in a common list, which also includes the notable LEEDS NO. 1, brought in by that Corporation. In view of their unconventional design, the two locomotives of Harrogate Corporation engaged on tunnel construction works are distinguished and treated last among the 2ft gauge locomotives, although their work was in the earlier part of the period.

HARROGATE   0-4-2 Saddle tank oc 6in x 10in, with outside bearings to the coupled wheels, by T Green & Son, of Leeds, 301 – ordered 6/1902 (at £450) and new 6/1902 for Harrogate waterworks. It was used for the Roundhill works (Harrogate). The *Yorkshire Post* of 1/1/1910 reported that G J Lockwood of 6 Princes Street, Harrogate offered for sale a 6in loco by T Green, 2ft gauge, presumed to be this one (the date aligns broadly with completion at Roundhill). Nevertheless, it probably stayed in the dale until 1913, as L R Perkins (employed by Arnolds at Leighton, 1910–14) well remembered its fatal accident, which occurred on 29/5/1911. It is known that on 4/10/1913 Arnolds acquired this loco from Arthur Atkinson of Masham (who contracted with the Corporations for various transport) and it was required by Arnolds at Stevenage. By 7/1914 the loco was at Arnolds' Doncaster yard; and still there (offered for sale) in 6/1919 but not listed by Arnolds in 7/1919; in 1920–21 it was with Arnolds at Melton cement works, near Hull; in 1922 it was at B Whitaker & Sons, Rothwell, a brickworks site – all these assignments believed to be for Arnolds, who may also have used it (finally?) at their John o' Gaunt quarry.

CLARO   0-4-2 Saddle tank oc 7in x 12in, with outside bearings to the coupled wheels and with close resemblance to HARROGATE, by T Green & Son, 312 – ordered 3/1903 (at £565) and new 3/1903 to Harrogate Corporation. The name is derived from the Wapentake (medieval administrative district) in which Harrogate was located and it was carried in raised brass letters on the sides of the tank. L R Perkins drove this loco for a time (in the dale) for Arnolds, who acquired it in 3/1911 and seemingly had it at Doncaster for overhaul in 7/1911. Edward Mills, who also drove for Arnolds, had charge of the loco during extension of Breary Banks camp, which would be early in the 1914 war. Following this, it went on to the building of filter beds near the racecourse in Boroughbridge Road, Ripon (concerned with a wartime camp), still for Arnolds. In the early nineteen-twenties it was on a contract of Arnolds, described as estate construction, at Kirk Sandall – and there is a hint of later use at a Middlesbrough ironworks; this allies with its ownership by John F Wake of Darlington and finally at Wake & Co's Port Clarence slag works.

MASHAM   0-6-2 Saddle tank oc 9½in by 14 in, outside bearings to coupled wheels by T Green & Son, 366, ordered 5/1904 (at £825) and new 9/1904 to Harrogate Corporation; shown by the makers despatched 'to E Wilson Dixon, Engineer for Harrogate Waterworks Railway, Masham, for Colsterdale Reservoirs'. The name was in raised letters on the tanks. It was bought for use on the main route of the 2ft gauge line, on its opening through from Roundhill and the depot at Leighton bridge all the way to Masham exchange yard with the North Eastern Railway. It shared the use of much of this route with LEEDS NO. 1 (to be described) and, after Harrogate finished their work (circa 1910), it was used on Leeds duties over the route, but acquired 15/5/1912 by Arnolds; this was apparently for an Asylum construction project, near Colchester, lasting 1912–14. Evidently back at the Belmont Sidings, Balby, Doncaster of H Arnold & Son, it was among plant advertised by auctioneers A T & E A Crow for sale on 14/6/1916. During 1916–17 it was also advertised by R H Longbottom, of Wakefield, machinery dealers. It must have gone into wartime service as, in *Surplus* of 1/4/1922, the Ministry of Munitions offered it for sale at Newbury; it was identified by its name, maker and gauge.

MASHAM would seem next to have found a home in wilder parts, the Cleveland hills, used by Pease & Partners at Upleatham ironstone mines – which Peases had operated since 1882. The mines were finally dismantled in 1924, by Watts, Hardy & Co. Ltd., of Newcastle upon Tyne; they advertised on 28/3/1924 (but without quoting location) mining machinery including '2ft 1in gauge loco No. 20, built by Green & Co. of Leeds, with 9¼in x 14in cylinders'. It is reasonable to judge that this was a survivor of the two 'two feet gauge' locomotives which Tom E Rounthwaite established as used by Peases on the tops at Upleatham but which he failed to identify. (Ref: *The Railway Observer* 6/1960 p.201).

By 8/1925, the loco was with Albert Batchelor Ltd, at Halling, on the Medway in Kent. Messrs. Stoyel and Kidner (*Cement Railways of Kent*) identify the site as a small cement works with the requisite quarry or 'pit' but they failed to establish its fate at Halling.

Harrogate Corporation's 2ft gauge MASHAM (T Green, 366 of 1904)

LEEDS NO. 1   0-6-2 Side tank oc 10¾in x 15in: outside Walschaerts gear and slide valves above the cylinders; outside bearings to the coupled wheels; 2ft 4in coupled wheels; weight in working order, 19 tons;

by Hunslet 865 of 1904 – new to Leeds Corporation, ex-works 24/1/1905, despatched to Masham. The livery as turned out was dark green, picked out black, with 'distant line' yellow, edged French grey, the buffer beams vermilion, and the painted title 'Leeds No. 1' being in gold on the tank sides. The claimed haulage capacity was 390 tons on the level, 110 tons up 1 in 50. It was a handsome engine, as evidenced by contemporary photographs and also by the fine model which appeared on public show in London, in January 1980, and now on show in the Birmingham Museum of Science and Industry.

Modifications to the locomotive were made in 1904–5; for these, and other aspects of the engine, see the main text, under the sub-head 'Railways for Leeds ... Masham to Colsterdale and Leighton'. After the departure of MASHAM in, probably, 1912, LEEDS NO. 1 was the only true main line locomotive in the dale. It worked all through the first world war, on military duties between Masham and Breary Banks, with its regular driver Tom Legge. Overhauled in 1919, it worked during the completion of Leighton reservoir.

Locomotive LEEDS No.1 in close-up

In this 'works view', the engine stands new, in plain grey. It is Hunslet 865 of 1904. Observe its outside framed trailing truck, as first constructed.

But on (it is believed) 30 September 1905, 'over she went', near Leighton Yard, after a slight misjudgment, while running light engine. The trailing truck has inside bearings, the form to which it had early been modified.

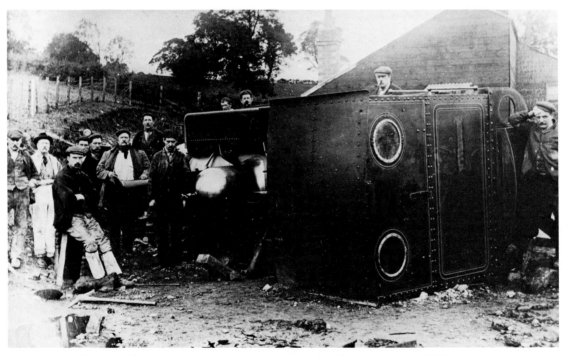

A companion view – and many 'companions in misfortune' – for LEEDS No.1.

Corporation minutes imply its ownership by Arthur Atkinson between 8/1908 and 5/1922; certainly all spares were ordered by Mr Atkinson between 1909 and the end of 1920. After its working career, Tom Legge, by then retired, polished it regularly in its shed at the exchange yard. As earlier mentioned, LEEDS NO. 1 was found at the exchange sidings on 6 June 1926. It was offered in the sale of 13 July 1926; and again offered in July 1928, by A Atkinson of Harrogate. Mr Humphrey Household visited Masham yard in late March 1928 and viewed the loco, now well sheeted, but on revisiting in the summer, he found that it had vanished.

Eventual disposal to Jack Head or Hird (of Hebburn-on-Tyne?) was suggested by Edward Mills, very knowledgeable on Colsterdale railways in their day. The only owner recorded by Hunslet Engine Company after Colsterdale times was John Shaw, Longhill, West Hartlepool, who is known to have been a scrap merchant in the nineteen-thirties.

LEEDS NO. 1 would be the engine which turned onto its side near Leighton bridge junction in September 1905 and the well-known photograph would be taken on that occasion.

SIDNEY 0-4-0 Well tank oc 5¾in x 10in

by Orenstein & Koppel, Berlin – thought on good authority to be their 1480 but (see deductions below) probably 1479; acquired 10/5/1912 by Arnolds from Orson Wright & Company, after use at their Ambergate pipeline site (*Manchester and the Peak*, pp.92/3). It was not the right gauge for Arnolds' Leighton lines but is recalled around 1912–14 on tip work and working on catchwater construction 'up Breary Banks way', thus in Colsterdale proper; the period is right for the construction of the catchwater from intake works on Spruce gill to Leighton.

It was recalled going on to Arnolds' Ripon camp job.

A comparable locomotive with nameplate SIDNEY on the front of the cab between the spectacle glasses was photographed in 1915 at Leeds Corporation's Knostrop sewage works, where it was on contract works. Its plate was deciphered as O & K 1478 or 1479. As 1478 was delivered new to Nancy, we are left with 1479 as probable identity for SIDNEY.

SIDNEY was on Arnolds' High Dyke construction contract for the Great Northern Railway, a job of 1915–19.

In 9/1919, SIDNEY lay at Doncaster available for sale by Arnolds. Arnolds however employed 2ft gauge tracks in course of building the Humber Cement Works at Melton, near Ferriby (beside the N.E.R. Selby–Hull line) in circa 1918–21 and SIDNEY was remembered arriving by trailer, traction engine hauled from Brough station, in 1919. It left the Melton site by 9/1921 and worked for Arnolds at Kirk Sandall, some five miles out of Doncaster, towards Hull. Pilkington Brothers' new glass works at Kirk Sandall opened in 1921 and involved site work by Arnolds; SIDNEY'S actual job has been linked with the (associated?) housing estate.

The 'tunnel locomotives', 2ft gauge, for Harrogate Corporation

MAY and PROGRESS: both were 0-4-0 oil-fired steam tank locomotives of special design, by German makers, and delivered for work in and out of a tunnel. Both locos carried plates reading:
'Arthur Koppel
27 Clements Lane
London E.C.'
who was the supplier, but not all locos supplied by Arthur Koppel were built by

Oil-fired steam locomotives, known as hydroleum locomotives, built in Germany and supplied by Arthur Koppel, used on 2ft gauge for Harrogate Corporation. They worked in and about the Carlesmoor aqueduct tunnel. PROGRESS is at the Fairthorne (Roundhill) end.

PROGRESS in close-up, at its shed, Fairthorne.

A footplate angle. Note the well for the driver's legs.

MAY – with its shed at the southerly end of Carlesmoor tunnel. This loco is distinguished by its protective roof and casing, but other distinctions from PROGRESS are discussed in the text.

The driver of MAY is seated comfortably, if snugly, on the 'footplate'.

MAY is now in countryside but, surprisingly, at the north end of Carlesmoor tunnel, the location identified by the hut and white wall. Roundhill reservoir house is to their left, hidden by a tree. The occasion may be on first delivery of the locomotive. If so, a considerable road journey will be needed to achieve delivery in the Laver valley.

Koppel of Berlin. Mr F Kemper (in *Industrial Railway Record* No. 44 of 1972 pp 286–8) states categorically that they were built by Arnold Jung, but is unable to identify them precisely in the records of Jung. An official photograph attributed to Jung depicts PROGRESS with the name on the tank as in its Harrogate days but with no Koppel (or other) plate below it – clearly a works view before leaving Jung to be sold by Koppel with his London plates. An 'official' photograph of MAY shows the name in the same large letters but also has the Koppel plate affixed below it. A catalogue of Arthur Koppel carries this illustration and records the loco as supplied for tunnel work on Harrogate Corporation's 2ft gauge railway.

The special features of these and broadly comparable German locos, known by their makers/suppliers as 'Hydroleum locomotives', were the use of oil firing in a water tube steam boiler of vertical format, with working steam pressure of 250 p.s.i., a multi-cylinder high speed steam engine and drive through chains and gearing to the leading axle, which in our two locos was coupled by conventional outside coupling rods to the trailing axle. Side tanks are carried and a right-hand view of PROGRESS suggests that water was held in the rear portion of the tanks and oil fuel in a forward compartment within the tanks; certainly water was delivered by a large horizontal boiler feed pump (to the right of the driver's seat and foot-well), while oil (of low grades) was pumped by a smaller pump (located on the right side of the frames near the front end) to the burners, this oil feed being automatically controlled so as to maintain the designed steam pressure in the boiler. The suppliers claimed that full pressure could be raised from cold in 15–20 minutes, although whether this was good practice one may doubt; if the boiler could adapt itself very speedily to fluctuations in demand, something like the flash boiler of a steam car, that would be valuable. The basic boiler design has been attributed to Serpollet (French engineer), going back to the late eighteen-eighties. The engine unit, said to have four cylinders and be based on steam launch practice (of the Hydroleum Company?), was mounted forward of the boiler; I had understood that the engine was vertical but comparison of pictures suggests that in PROGRESS it is horizontal (transversely mounted?) and with only two cylinders whereas MAY could have a vertical engine and conceivably with four cylinders. MAY had a more enclosed front end, as illustrated, and side access doors near the front end. Both locos are seen to have a puny regulator handle entering the upper part of the boiler unit. Probably the control placed low on the driver's left (lever and ratchet on PROGRESS and pull-out rod on MAY) would be for notching up and reversing; the valvegear is concealed in all pictures. MAY ran with a roof extending its full length, supported on uprights at the four corners of the loco and the aspect is of a steam tram engine, but without external condenser. PROGRESS had a similar roof in the Jung photograph but is depicted in service without a cab. In some respects, the conception and design ante-date the well known Sentinel steam railway locomotive, although that in turn borrowed from its makers' road loco practice. The only minute of probable relevance which has been traced is one recording the decision, in February 1904, to purchase a small steam engine, price £187, to haul material in and out of the tunnel.

Both locomotives were recalled working in conjunction with the boring of the major tunnel which carries the water from Roundhill reservoir, in a south easterly direction, under Clint Crags, on an alignment indicated today by the sighting tower on the crags. PROGRESS worked from the northern (Roundhill) end and could run into the heading, while MAY had a shed at the southern (Carlesmoor) end. Its surface route is mentioned in the text. A picture in a Koppel catalogue illustrates it hauling four metal side-tipping trucks, full of stone, sand or aggregates, across a rough pasture and onto a stone-built embankment, with woodland on the hill slope in the near background. These two intriguing locomotives and their work were before the days of most informants met in the dale in time past but Tom Garth associated Jack Cattel (a distant relation) with PROGRESS, probably maintaining it in its shed at Roundhill. On completion of the tunnel, what became of MAY and PROGRESS?

Imeson & Jopling offered to sell on 5 August 1910, at Roundhill Waterworks, for Harrogate Corporation … plant including two 10hp locomotives by Arthur Koppel fed by oil fuel, 2ft gauge. (*Contract Journal*, 27/7/1910). In the same Journal, issue 24/1/1917, J Wardell & Company, dealers, London, offered plant including … two 2ft gauge hydroleum locomotives. The reference in 1910 will assuredly be to MAY and PROGRESS. That of January 1917 is likely to be to the same pair, but with no clue given to their location at the time.

If these 2ft gauge locomotives achieved sale in 1917, it would almost certainly be for constructional work backed by the Ministry of Munitions (MM) of those days. Such a project was 'the Oldham Aircraft Factory', constructed between January and November 1918 on sites to both sides of the L&YR Manchester–Rochdale (and Bradford/Leeds/Wakefield) main line immediately beyond Moston station when en route to Yorkshire. The buildings were firstly for assembly of Handley Page bomber aircraft to be received from manufacture in U.S.A., with also hangars for the aircraft when completed, and an airfield was constructed for their commissioning tests. Trollope & Colls Ltd. were the main contractors for constructing these works, which came to a sudden stop in November 1918. Advertisements appeared in *Contract Journal* under dates 12/2/1919, 26/3/1919, 4/6/1919 and 6/8/1919 – with Trollope & Colls Ltd and auctioneers G N Dixon seeking to sell '2ft gauge Jubilee track and two Jubilee locos, fitted with Sentinel boilers', elaborated progressively to indicate that the two locomotives were steam locos by Koppel, rebuilt with Sentinel type boilers, one of 2ft gauge and the other quoted after the first announcement as being a Hydroleum locomotive by Koppel on 1ft 8in gauge. It seems that at 26/3/1919 there were also a pair of Hudson locos (made by?) for 2ft gauge but that these more conventional machines soon sold. The rarities probably failed to sell.

MAY is now working in unexpectedly open surroundings, surely on its way with a load from the stone quarry in the secluded Laver valley to the south end of Carlesmoor tunnel.

Locomotives (steam), 3ft gauge, of Harold Arnold & Son ('Limited' from 28/7/1916) employed on the Leighton reservoir project of Leeds Corporation – for which the contract was placed on 1/7/1908, and suspended 1/4/1915.

It is thought that, during over thirty years of research, a complete list of steam locomotives on the project at Leighton has been compiled. They are grouped according to their builders: Peckett & Sons Limited, of Bristol; W G Bagnall Limited, of Stafford; Hudswell Clarke & Company Limited, of Leeds. The individual dates of arrival on site have not been ascertained.

SWANSEA   0-4-0 Saddle tank oc 8in x 12in
by Peckett 959 of 1902 – had been new 5/1902 to Swansea Corporation for Cray reservoir and used there until, probably, 1905 or 1906. It was acquired by Arnolds, who just possibly used it for a time at Embsay Moor reservoir, near Skipton, and certainly employed it at Castle Carrock reservoir, near Brampton (until, probably, 1909); used by Arnolds at Leighton and later on their military camp construction at Ripon and railway building at Colsterworth, Great Northern Railway. By 4/1919, known as 5 SWANSEA, this loco was with Cafferata & Co. Ltd, Newark, broken up there in 1947.

LEIGHTON   0-4-0 Saddle tank oc 10in x 14in
by Peckett 968 of 1902 – had been new to Heywood and Middleton Water Board and used at Ashworth Moor reservoir, with the local name CHEESDEN (nameplate on tank); sold from there 19/5/1909; it is believed that J B Watson & Son of Leeds were intermediaries; acquired by Arnolds in or by 18/5/1911 and worked at Leighton, now named LEIGHTON. It was still Arnolds' property in 10/1914 and may have stayed with them on 1914–18 wartime works. After the war, it was with Nott Brodie & Co. Ltd at Blaen-y-Cwm, near Beaufort, job of c. 1918–22, and sold from there to Taf Fechan Water Supply Board in 6/1922 for the Taf Fechan reservoir job at Pontsticill; for sale there in 9/1927 and later with A R Adams of Newport and Curran Brothers of Cardiff. The name LEIGHTON was retained at Blaen-y-Cwm and Taf Fechan.

GILL   0-4-0 Saddle tank oc 8in x 12in
by Peckett 1003 of 1903 – new 6/1903 to Fisher & le Fanu, at Goulds Cross, as CASHEL. On coming over from Ireland, it may have worked for them in the period c. 1907–09 on filter bed construction at Bamford, Derbyshire (*Manchester and the Peak*, pp. 88/90). It was acquired on 15/2/1912 by Arnolds from J B Watson & Son for use at Leighton. It presumably went on to Arnolds' wartime jobs and in 9/1919 it lay (as GILL) at their Doncaster yard, available for sale. Peckett 1003 was still with Arnolds in 10/1923. It was with Harris and Lewis Welfare and Development Company, at Leverburgh, in 1924 (cf PENWYLLT, below); and subsequently with A M Carmichael ('8') on Scots projects, and sold by him for scrap in 1950.

BURN   0-4-0 Wing (inverted saddle) tank oc 9in x 13½in
by W G Bagnall 902 of 1887 – had been new 5/1887 to contractor H Fotherby at Cant Clough reservoir, near Burnley, as VICTORIA, and subsequently used elsewhere by Fotherby; it was with Benjamin Lumb, at Gorpley reservoir, near Todmorden, as TODMORDEN, in c. 1900–04. Arnolds had it on their Embsay Moor job, Skipton, still as TODMORDEN, with which name it is remembered coming to Leighton, but it became BURN at Leighton, named after the local river. It was with Arnolds for (at least) the years 1909–13 but its later history has not been traced by its makers. It was thought in the dale that it passed to Leeds Corporation, by whom (it was suggested) it was broken up fairly soon after Arnolds' departure. I discount a suggestion that WGB 902 was with Yorkshire contractors Crabtree Brothers in earlier years.

Here we retrieve from the author's *Bowland Forest and Craven Country*, the striking view there presented at p.61. The locomotive was erroneously identified as MARY, although correctly placed in Embsay village. Note the unusual dome, for a Bagnall-built loco. It is now believed to be REDE by Bagnall 1413 of 1894 and maybe leaving Embsay Moor contract of Harold Arnold for loan to Sir John Jackson in the wilds of Rannoch Moor – but to come south a couple of years later to Leighton reservoir site, where REDE was employed by Arnold.

This is Bagnall 1413 of 1894 at a cement site in Kent in the 1920s. Note the dome, for comparison with the Embsay scene of years before.

REDE	0-4-0 Saddle tank oc 9in x 14in

by W G Bagnall 1413 dated 1892 – had been delivered from the maker's stock in 3/1894 or 4/1894, via agents, to the Newcastle & Gateshead Water Company on the Catcleugh reservoir project. Spares for the loco were ordered by J B Watson & Son (machinery dealers, of Leeds) in 1906 and in 4/1908 by Sir John Jackson, who doubtless used it on their hydro-electric construction works for the British Aluminium Company, at Kinlochleven and on Rannoch moor, job of 1907–10. The loco came to Arnolds by 12/1909 for Leighton and retained its original name (after a river in Northumberland) at this site. It was still Arnolds' property in 8/1913 and went on to their camp construction at Ripon.

If the Bagnall locomotive with a surprising bell-mouthed dome illustrated by me in *Bowland and Craven*, plate 61, is REDE (as is now suspected) it may have first joined Arnolds at Embsay Moor c. 2/1906 and been released on loan to Jacksons in 1908. In 1920, this loco reached the South Metropolitan Gas Company at their Old Kent Road works, was found too large for the restricted clearances and was resold in 1921 to (so it is said) British Fibrocement Works Co. Ltd (Turners Asbestos Co. Ltd) at Erith, Kent. However, in 1921, the loco named REDE passed to A.P.C.M. Ltd at Swanscombe cement works, Kent, where it was necessarily altered to 3ft 5½in gauge with outside wheel flanges. A photograph at this site shows an obvious Bagnall loco (without cab at that time) with a huge dome and twin spring balance safety valve columns appended. After this, REDE disappears from view, probably laid aside in 1927 and shortly broken up.

NIDD	0-4-0 Saddle tank oc 8in x 12in

by W G Bagnall 1658 of 1902 – had been new 7/1902 to Holme & King at Pateley Bridge and used in upper Nidderdale, whence acquired by Arnolds, by 3/1909, for Leighton; it was recalled being brought over the moors from Lofthouse by horse haulage, relieved in the later stages of the journey by an Atkinson-owned traction engine. It suffered a fatal disaster in the quarry above Leighton, on 3/5/1911, being badly damaged and reputedly broken up. In fact, the makers provided a new chimney to Arnolds for it, 25/5/1911 and NIDD was repaired and resumed work on site, but not in the quarry. Unlike the other locos of Arnolds (apart, perhaps, from BURN) it passed to Leeds Corporation. It lay at Masham, a candidate for sale, in 6/1926, but I have not traced it further.

There is scope for confusion of identity. Bagnall 1423 of 1893, this engine a 'wing' tank, was employed on Bradford's waterworks of 1893–96 at Grimwith and then with John Best of Leith on Edinburgh's Talla aqueduct construction, as THE DUKE. On Bests' work in upper Nidderdale it acquired the name NIDD, seemingly while our other NIDD was working on much the same tracks. WGB 1423 went on to Sir John Jackson Ltd, Kinlochleven and became their property; it was in a sales inventory of theirs in 1921.

CRAY	0-4-0 Saddle tank oc 7in x 12in

by W G Bagnall 1674 of 1901 – had been new to Swansea Corporation at Cray reservoir site, in 12/1901. After that job, it was with James Byrom from the latter half of 1906 at Scout Moor, near Edenfield, until c. 1909. It was believed to come to Arnolds about that time, at Leighton, although it was the only one of their main series of 3ft gauge locos at Leighton never recalled to me personally. Corroboration? Indeed, the makers' books suggest it remained with Byrom at 15/7/1914.

PENWYLLT	0-4-0 Saddle tank oc 7in x 12in

by W G Bagnall 1704 of 1902 – had been new to Swansea Corporation at Cray, in

12/1902, with this name; still there 10/1905 but by 3/1906 it was with Arnolds. It was recalled to have come direct from South Wales to Leighton but it is likely to have been the Bagnall loco with 7in cylinders used by Arnolds at Castle Carrock, a job near Brampton of 1906–09, before moving on to Leighton. After 1914 or 1915, it presumably did wartime work for Arnolds and was recorded at their Doncaster depot in 1919 (still as PENWYLLT when advertised there in 8/1919) and 1923. In late 1924 it was with Harris and Lewis Welfare and Development Co. Ltd (Lord Leverhulme's Company, formed 11/1919) at Leverburgh, Isle of Harris, where the harbour and industrial scheme collapsed in 1925. By 1926, it belonged to A M Carmichael, Edinburgh contractors, at Uphall station yard; reported seen 6/1934 stored at Drumnadrochit, Inverness-shire, on Carmichael's North Road contract; later, probably finally, at the firm's Corstorphine depot, being broken up sometime after 1938.

POTT   0-4-0 Saddle tank oc 9in x 15in (approximately)
by Hudswell Clarke 311 of 1889 – had been new to one William Perch of Cwm Clydach colliery, Swansea Vale, with the name CLYDACH, and had been converted from his narrower gauge of 2ft 10in, evidently not too successfully, as it had a reputation for coming off the road at Leighton. Before its Leighton days it had been in the hands of C D Phillips, Newport dealer (1899) and by 1900 those of contractors Abraham Kellett & Sons, on the Elan valley pipeline to Birmingham, with the name HAGLEY. It can be tentatively identified in Kelletts' sale of 5/1908 at Hayfield (*Manchester and the Peak*, p.46) and one may note that his locos are usually quoted as 2ft 9in gauge. Arnolds secured it during 1908, by November, and from recollections it was probably the first of his locos at Leighton site. It acquired its local name after coming and was still at Leighton in 6/1913. After its work at Leighton, a better job was made of converting POTT to 3ft gauge; significantly, it carried in later life a plate recording its rebuilding by Arnolds in 1915. It went on to Arnolds' Colsterworth contract.
This loco was on Nott Brodie's Blaen-y-Cwm reservoir job of c. 1918–22. It was sold from there in 6/1922 to Taf Fechan Water Supply Board, worked at Taf Fechan, Pontsticill, and was for sale there in 9/1927, its name being NEWPORT; Nott had ordered spares at Newport in 1921 – maybe indicating an interlude on dock work? Phillips evidently had the engine again, as he sold it in 4/1929 to the Forest of Dean Stone Firms Ltd, at Porthgain in extreme West Wales, where it worked and, after disuse, was eventually broken up around 9/1953.

BRIGG   0-4-0 Saddle tank oc 9in x 15in
by Hudswell Clarke 504 of 1898 – new 10/1899 for Newcastle & Gateshead Water Company, who used the loco on their Catcleugh construction; a place name local to these works is 'Brig' but this engine always seems to have carried the name in Lincolnshire style. Its career c. 1905–11 is obscure but, through the good offices of London dealers J Wardell & Company, it found its way to Arnolds, by 12/2/1912 and worked at Leighton. Its wartime period concluded with sale by the Ministry of Munitions in 1919 to the Abertillery Water Board, for employment at Grwyne Fawr, in the Black Mountains. BRIGG went direct in 1928 from this site to Lehane, Mackenzie & Shand, being their HESWALL at Gorple, Fernilee and Darley Dale yard (see *Yorkshire Pennines* p.B126, and *Manchester and the Peak*, p.58).

HEALEY   0-4-0 Saddle tank oc 9in x 15in
by Hudswell Clarke 1038 of 1914 – coming as a new engine, ex-works 31/1/1914 to Arnolds, for Leighton, soon going to the Ripon and Colsterworth contracts and later it was in Arnolds' Doncaster yard as a pump boiler, being sold in 8/1927

through the agency of T W Ward Ltd to Lehane, Mackenzie & Shand, their GORPLE at Brownhill, Gorple and Fernilee; then with Richard Baillie on his Ladybower contract in Derbyshire, which extended from 1936 to 1946 (*Yorkshire Pennines*, p.B126; *Manchester and the Peak*, pp 58 and 103).

The initial name was after the village, near Leighton.

FEARBY 0-4-0 Saddle tank oc 9in x 15in

by Hudswell Clarke 1085 of 1914 – coming new to Arnolds, ex-works 12/6/1914, and having a similar history to HEALEY right down, it is said, to stationary use at Doncaster. It was sold direct (but through Wards' agency) in 7/1927 from Arnolds Doncaster depot to Hayes (Stockport) Ltd, at Elslack reservoir contract for Barnoldswick; and sold from there to Nelson Corporation as their No. 2 at Coldwell reservoir, 1929–36, or later. Soon after this, it was acquired by Sir Lindsay Parkinson, public works contractors, who engaged in construction of Royal Ordnance Factories during the next few years and then increasingly in opencast coal getting. In their hands, the loco figured as SIR ANTHONY EDEN. As late as 5/1946, it lay at Winwick, still property of 'S.L.P.'. The original name derived from Fearby village, near Leighton.

Locomotives (steam), 3ft gauge, of Leeds Corporation, employed on Leighton reservoir construction and associated works.

Arnagill quarry was reopened in 1922, now by Leeds Corporation as successors to Arnolds, after its wartime disuse. In that autumn suitable second-hand steam locomotives were being sought, to work on the 3ft gauge tracks left behind by Arnolds in the quarry area. Two were acquired, both built in 1917 by Kerr Stuart, of Stoke-on-Trent, to their 'Haig' class (of which 3083 was the prototype; it was temporarily named HAIG when new and photographed as such at Stoke). The locomotives were –

0-6-0 Side tank oc 8½in x 11in, with Walschaerts gear and slide valves above the cylinders

by Kerr Stuart 3083 of 1917 – had been new 16/10/1917 to the Board of Trade's Home Grown Timber Committee, intended for the Canadian Forestry Corps, Wandsworth Road Depot (via Stewarts Lane, South Eastern and Chatham Railway) as CTS 4 – thought to have been based at Masham on wartime forestry work and this may have been its first assignment.

After essential completion of work at Leighton reservoir by Leeds Corporation, it was noted by Mr J W Armstrong lying at Masham exchange sidings, without name or number but with plate KS 3083 of 1917, on 6/6/1926, shortly before the sale of 7/1926 – but any later history is lacking.

0-6-0 Side tank oc 8½in x 11in, similar to the preceding loco, by Kerr Stuart 3084 of 1917 – had been new to the B.O.T. Committee, 19/11/1917, to be sent by the makers via Ampthill station, Midland Railway, to 126 Company, Canadian Forestry Corps, as CTS 5 – also possibly based at Masham on forestry work.

After the Leighton works, it was not in evidence to Mr Armstrong on his visits to the dale and exchange sidings, but it was acquired by Lehane, Mackenzie & Shand, contractors, becoming their CARDIFF; it worked at Gorple reservoir (job of 1927–34) and (briefly) Fernilee, also for the Admiralty in Orkney, and it survived the second world war (*Yorkshire Pennines* p.B125 and *Manchester and the Peak* p.57).

One of the two foregoing quarry locomotives was said to have been wrecked in a runaway around 1924–25 and broken up by the Corporation, while the other was to be offered for sale in 1926. It is thus strange that the one *not* in evidence in 6/1926 has a well-authenticated later history from about 1927 onwards.

The suggestion that the two locos above quoted worked in wartime at forestry sites near *Masham* derives from pencilled entries in their makers' books and must be treated with reserve. To confuse matters, a third similar loco had 'Masham' pencilled in as a seeming forestry assignment. This was Kerr Stuart 3085 of 1917, CTS 6 of the Forestry Corps. It was at least nominally consigned new to Dornoch station, Highland Railway. It was sold from Forestry Corps stock c. 1922 to Alexander Hammond, an intermediary in Slough, and soon went on to a career in ironstone country, so was not a candidate for Leeds Corporation ownership, nor for work or demise at Arnagill quarry.

From the list of 3ft gauge locomotives employed by Harold Arnold & Son at or about Leighton site in the 1908–15 era, it will be observed that two locomotives were seemingly left behind at Leighton when Arnolds removed their plant in 1914–15. They were –

BURN   0-4-0 Wing (inverted saddle) tank oc 9in x 13½in
             by W G Bagnall 902 of 1887.
             Broken up shortly by Leeds Corporation?
             No evidence of employment in the era of activity from 1922 onwards.

NIDD   0-4-0 Saddle tank oc 8in x 12in
             by W G Bagnall 1658 of 1902
             Passed to Leeds Corporation.
             Lay at Masham exchange sidings 6/6/1926, on the occasion of Mr J W Armstrong's
             visit, but not clearly offered for sale 7/1926.

Kerr Stuart of Stoke-on-Trent built their 3083 of 1917, prototype of their Haig class, for use in wartime Britain by the Canadian Forestry Corps. This locomotive was acquired in due time by Leeds Corporation for use around Leighton reservoir, on the 3ft gauge tracks which Arnolds had put in before the war. Leeds also secured a second of these engines for use at Leighton.

Chapter Five

Kirkby Malzeard Light Railway

It may be recalled that Leeds Corporation secured their initial Act for reservoirs at Colsterdale, Leighton, Carlesmoor and Laverton in 1901; the main aqueduct, Leighton–Kirkby Malzeard–Kettlesing dates from 1907–11, Kettlesing tunnel from 1903–09.

In February 1904, Ripon Rural District Council wrote to the waterworks committee of Leeds Corporation asking assistance in obtaining a light railway from Ripon to Kirkby Malzeard, but the committee were unwilling to assist. Nevertheless, a project was developed and formally put forward in May 1906 under the title of the Kirkby Malzeard Light Railway. Promoters were Messrs Ellis, Richmond, Cathcart, Bland, Mossman and Admiral Oxley, some being landowners on the route and the first three named as directors. The engineer was Edward Wilson Dixon, M.I.C.E., of 3, East Parade, Leeds. The route of nearly six miles (5 miles, 7 furlongs, 5½ chains to be precise) commenced alongside the N.E.R. (Leeds Northern line) on the west side, a little to the north of Ripon station. Trains would leave from the south end of the Light Railway site and immediately negotiate a curve of 264ft radius in order to head westwards for most of the route.

The river Ure was to be crossed by a major bridge. Three significant roads and several lanes had to be crossed and all by level crossings. The Masham road was crossed beyond the northern outskirts of Ripon. The next road was crossed immediately south of Straw House. Birkby Nab was a little south of the route, likewise Cow Myers (with Hollin Head Wood to its north). The Azerley road was crossed north of Galphay village. After another road crossing, the line would turn north and end south of Kirkby Malzeard, roughly a half mile short of the village centre and about the same distance from Laverton. West of the Ure bridge, the line would climb at 1 in 20 and the Ministry Inspector suggested easing this to 1 in 25 (presumably involving a cutting) and carrying the Masham road over the line by a bridge. Some other gradients were as steep as 1 in 18 and 1 in 25, mostly unfavourable to westerly travel, as the outer terminus would be about 400ft above that at Ripon. Nowhere would the Light Railway be nearer than 1½ miles to the centre of Ripon. Its route was highly rural in character.

The proposal was for a 3ft gauge line. The Ministry would have preferred 2ft 6in (influence of Calthrop here?) but the Light Railway Order of 1907 was confirmed 6 May 1907, with permission for 3ft (or other gauge with the consent of the Minister).

From their detailed estimates in 1906, it is clear that Leeds Water Works department had in mind the possibility of providing traffic and revenue for the Light Railway for a period of 12 years; this was to arise primarily in connection with the proposed Laverton reservoir works – and one would think also those on Carlesmoor reservoir construction. However, the waterworks committee simply took note and determined to watch the interests of the city. As we know, they never proceeded with their Carlesmoor and Laverton schemes and they heard no more until March 1920, when the Reverend R Vardy wrote of a scheme to extend the standard gauge light railway from Ripon Military Camp to Kirkby Malzeard. The camp has been mentioned in connection with Arnolds' contracts early in the war, when their work at Leighton was run down and suspended. The branch line to the camp left the N.E.R. at Littlethorpe signal box, nearly two miles south of Ripon station, and took a westerly course over the Harrogate–Ripon main road, the layout within the camp area (west of the main road) being quite extensive; the War Department or Ministry of Munitions evidently provided some motive power, as John W Armstrong once saw 'Inland Docks and Waterways No. 52', which he recognised as a 4-4-0 Tank engine one time of the Midland & Great Northern Railway. The N.E.R. sent No. 972, class 'E' 0-6-0 Tank locomotive, fresh from overhaul at Darlington Works, in July 1916. No. 1789 of the same type was also reported here and, before the site closed down in the 1920s, class 'E' locomotives from Starbeck shed were normally employed, although not necessarily penetrating to all parts of the camp layouts.

The scheme of 1920 would evidently have given Kirkby Malzeard a standard gauge line, approaching from the south. Later in 1920, the Town Clerk of Ripon suggested the formation of a committee to explore the project. The waterworks committee, by then substantial landowners in the Laver valley, realised that a light railway could help their tenant farmers and others but they declined to give financial support or participate in discussions. Kirkby Malzeard has never yet achieved a railway terminus.

Ripon and District Light Railways, with a Light Railway Order secured 22 June 1904, would be a project broadly contemporary with the first plans for a Nidd Valley Light Railway in upper Nidderdale – over the hills – and the N.V.L.R. was first proposed in 2ft 6in gauge form with L.R.O. 31 March 1901. The Ripon and District scheme of 1904 (never constructed) has also been attributed to Power & Traction Ltd, with a route to run about 2½ miles out of Ripon on the road to Nidderdale, which road was crossed by the military railway of later date.

A scene on 18 April 1907 at Headingley filter beds construction. The foundations of the meter house are in the foreground and one sees the south east corner of the site, bounded by the main Otley Road (L to R) and Church Wood Avenue (to right). The houses on the far (east) side of Otley Road remain prominent today, with Glen Road in the gap between them. Otley Road had not yet become a tramway route at this point in 1907. A traction engine, thought to be by McLaren of Leeds, is seen to have brought a truck of bricks, the side being lowered to display the load. The bricks may be transferred to the flat truck on the temporary railway track.

Chapter Six

Transport by City Tramways

As already indicated, the waters from the Washburn valley reservoirs at Fewston and Swinsty (later augmented from Leighton and Thruscross) are conveyed by aqueducts to the storage reservoir at Eccup. Thence, they pass by the parallel Alwoodley or Blackmoor tunnels to the 'Seven Arches' (Adel) and pipelines onwards to filter beds at Weetwood and Headingley. The Weetwood beds, on the east side of Otley Road, were developed in the nineteenth century. In 1906–11, the Headingley beds, to the west of Otley Road, were constructed, and the road is believed to have been widened at the same time.

Until a few years before these waterworks developments in the north western residential outskirts of Leeds, street tramways for passengers, with horse and steam traction, were in use, as also pioneer electric operation from as early as 1892–95. Electric cars were running to Headingley, some three miles out of town, in 1906 but only as far as the Headingley depot, which in turn was on the same site as its predecessor. An extension of tramway route, electrified from the outset, was made from Headingley Depot to West Park and commissioned 11 September 1908, this used the rising stretch of Otley Road which passes between the older Weetwood beds and the Headingley beds, these latter being:–

1. Four beds and a clear water tank by C Bushby & Sons, 1906–09; and
2. Six beds – by Holme & King, of Liverpool, 1909–11

Various materials would be required for the new works and one might expect bricks, cement, crushed stone, sand and gravel to predominate, plus valves, fittings, meters and the like.

It was agreed in January 1906 between the tramways and water committees of Leeds Corporation that the former would convey material from the North Eastern Railway's depot in Cardigan Road to the new filter beds, at 1/3d per ton; the general manager of the tramways department was to carry out the necessary siding and other works and the water department to arrange for loading and unloading of traffic. Cardigan Road goods yard (closed 4 September 1972) was bounded on the west by the N.E.R. Leeds Northern line (a little south of the modern Burley Park passenger station) and on the east by Cardigan Road. If a siding were connected from the yard into the tram tracks, the route to Headingley would be northward along Cardigan Road, but diversion by Victoria Road to Hyde Park Corner (Leeds!) and reversal there to go by the main Headingley Lane and Otley Road would have been necessary – as the more direct tramway link by North Lane was not available until the 1920s. The question of motive power on the tramway is intriguing. Perhaps service cars of the Corporation electric stock could have been employed. Great fun would be to find a couple of the City's retired steam tram engines by T Green (whom we have noted building 2ft gauge locomotives for Colsterdale in 1902–04) and have them sneak out of the N.E.R. yard nocturnally and so to Headingley while the good citizens slept; the passenger service would not be disrupted.

It is however clear that for at least a couple of years a temporary extension of about ½ mile would have been required to the tramtracks and no evidence has been traced of such a temporary extension. Indeed, it is believed that the use of the street tramways was not achieved during 1906–09. There are nevertheless pointers to transport arrangements. On 15 December 1906 the N.E.R. minuted commencement of the 'Leeds service from Cardigan Road for new filter beds, conveying building material' and N.E.R. historian Kenneth Hoole felt that this pointed to use of a N.E.R. steam wagon. On 11 February 1907 the City Highways committee requested the Town Clerk to give 'the necessary notice' to the Railway Company to terminate the committee's tenancy of railway sidings at Cardigan Road depot. Photographs were taken at the Headingley filters site on 18 April 1907. One of these depicts a steam lorry which could well be of the 'Yorkshire' make with transverse boiler; it carries lining and lettering but is too distant for this to be read. In the background are the site huts (doubtless offices and stores) just inside from the Otley Road at probably a midpoint on the main road frontage. An excavated filter bed is in the foreground and there are narrow gauge light tracks and metal tip wagons to run on them. The second picture of the same date shows in the foreground the newly made foundations for the meter house at the south east corner of the site. A large two-cylinder compound steam traction engine has drawn off the road onto the site, hauling a trailer load of bricks, the side of the trailer lowered for display of the load. The engine is thought to be of McLaren (of Leeds) make and incidentally to be larger than any owned by the N.E.R. A flat wagon stands on a short length of narrow gauge track, more or less between the trailer and the site of the structure. Glen Road is behind the engine, on the far side of the main road, and the familiar houses in gardens on Otley Road are much as today. No tramway wires are to be seen. It is probable that steam lorries and traction engine haulage of road trailers brought all requirements to site during 1906–09.

Reporting on the year to 31 March 1910, the water committee note that Holme & King Ltd of Liverpool were actively engaged on constructing their six filter beds, with the substantial average of 89 men and 38 horses employed. The report of one year later records that Holme & King had practically finished. The 'tramways and electricity' committee and the waterworks committee

A scene around 1910–1911, with the filter beds near completion. This is also looking eastward to Otley Road but slightly further north on the site and with the main gates opening from the filter site to the main road. The standard gauge electrified tramway of Leeds Corporation by this time passes along Otley Road and a branch siding can be made out, entering the gates and becoming 'mixed gauge' to facilitate delivery of sand and gravel for use in the filter beds.

came together in June 1910 when the tenders of Mr J L Micklethwaite for supply of gravel and A Braithwaite & Company (? being Mr Micklethwaite's Company) to supply sand were related to handling arrangements at Sovereign Street depot. Evidently the sand and gravel would each be conveyed by the River Aire to a wharf in the vicinity of the City Tramways' Swinegate works and depot, virtually in the shadow of Leeds 'New' (later 'City') station viaducts. The tramways committee were responsible for making sidings, providing rolling stock and conveyance to the filters site. The need for 'overhead material' was also noted and total expenditure was estimated at £5,000. Included was an electric crane and grab, from Booth Brothers, and seven trucks (meaning wheelsets, etc, tramcar style) and seven sets of motors and controllers, all from Dick Kerr & Company, and hoppers for seven wagons, these to come from Robert Hudson. Hudsons' advertisement is reproduced and is probably 'touched up' from a Leeds Corporation Tramways photograph. Observe the overhead trolley collection from the wires, and premises in background. Conveyance of coal from Harehills pit (north east Leeds) to the Headingley filters by tramway tippler cars has also been mentioned. (A little surprisingly, the date 1908 was associated with this movement). A photograph at site showing beds well advanced illustrates standard gauge track entering the site off the Otley road and through the main permanent gates, with overhead power conductor. From the internal s.g. tramway siding transhipment was clearly made to a portable narrow gauge complex. No motive power or other rolling stock appears on the view.

This is an electric tramway tippler car of the type supplied by Robert Hudson of Leeds, incorporating electrical and running gear by Dick Kerr & Company – in the first instance employed to convey sand and gravel from a wharf on the River Aire at Sovereign Street in central Leeds by way of the City Tramways, to reach Headingley site.

Thus we have the satisfaction of knowing that tramway haulage was employed, albeit probably only in 1910–11. The water committee noted on 17 November 1911 that at the new filter beds the engine and boiler had been sold for £90 to T W Ward Ltd and the remainder of the plant to G Wilson & Company for £161. What became of the (nocturnally employed?) tramway tipper fleet after 1911? It is understood that examples survived over 30 years! A metal memorial tablet was to be affixed and the committee visited the filters on 19 April 1912. In April 1986, the handsome plaque, with city arms, was found recently restored and installed on the stairway central to the modern office and laboratory block at Headingley filters site, now seemingly included under the title of Weetwood. Among names perpetuated are those of Charles C Henzell, M.Inst.C.E., waterworks engineer, and William Nicholson as Lord Mayor. Completion of the ten beds is recorded as December 1911.

This photo and the one reproduced opposite are scenes of 24 November 1919 and carry their contemporary inscriptions. They show an ex-Ministry of Munitions/War Department 60cm (2ft) gauge internal combustion locomotive, still with its W.D. number plate 2835, as when these locos were in use behind the front lines on the Western Front. The loco is in use on the waterworks project for laying an additional line of pipes from Seven Arches (Adel) to Weetwood filter beds at Headingley. The location is likely to parallel Weetwood Lane.

A further development

An additional line of pipes from Seven Arches (Adel) to Weetwood filter beds was laid, 42in diameter and made of reinforced concrete. A tender was accepted on 28 September 1914, but suspended. Work of excavation and laying was resumed in earnest on 12 January 1920, under Corporation engineer A S Hamilton, vice C Watson, resigned. (Mr Hamilton was a good friend, helpfully recalling and illustrating the layout in Colsterdale). In April 1920, our friends Harold Arnold & Son Ltd were called in to construct approximately 140 yards of driftway under the property of Mr M Mannaberg.

This project seems to have shared with Colsterdale in employment of rails, tipping wagons and petrol locomotives from Ministry of Munitions/War Department disposals of surplus light railway equipment. The neighbourhood of the pipeline is that traversed by Weetwood Lane.

Reproduced are two photographs dated 24 November 1919, evidently taken as preparations were made for the job. Ex-W.D.L.R. locomotive No. 2835 is attractively displayed and the view with top casing removed is presumed to be of the opposite side of the same locomotive. I have failed to locate the dignified residence depicted in the background, although broadly comparable houses border Weetwood Lane.

A view of WDLR 2835 with its cover removed. Note starting handle!

Chapter Seven

Reservoirs and Railways for the City of Bradford

Introduction

Among Britain's most exciting projects of waterworks engineering in 'the age of steam' were those of Bradford and its contractors at Upper Barden (1876–1882) and subsequently in Nidderdale (1890–1937). Railways played a major part in these projects. Before studying these lines and their locations it is interesting to go back in time and secure a broader perspective – taking in, briefly, the period 1843 to circa 1875, during which 'pick and shovel' techniques prevailed, essentially without railways.

The Waterworks Company

The Bradford Waterworks Company, undertaking works of 1843–1855, could supply water to premises up to about 520ft o.d. from their town reservoir at *Wheatley Hill*. Advised by Thomas Hawksley, noted London consultant engineer, they built *Upper Chellow Dene reservoir*, capacity about 50 million gallons, and this was completed by January 1853. They proposed to seek powers for new works in the parliamentary session 1852–53.

At this time, however, the City Council looked for a more ambitious scheme and consulted John Frederic la Trobe Bateman, of Manchester, whose preliminary report was presented in October 1852. The Council went to Parliament and by the Bradford Water Works Act, 1854, took over the Company's properties and set to work on a programme of expansion.

Projects carried out or designed until 1863

This was the era as engineer of John W Leather, of Leeds.

Hewenden and *Upper* and *Lower Chellow* reservoirs (not to be confused with the later *Chellow Heights*) were formed, with *Globe* or *Wheatley Hill* at the town end of the supply line.

There followed *Grimwith* (compensation), *Lower Barden*, *Chelker*, *Silsden* and – at the town end of the aqueduct – *Heaton* reservoirs. The contractors have been quoted as Duckitt & Stead for *Grimwith* and *Heaton*, Mr Buxton for *Chelker* and *Silsden* and Blair & Parrett for *Lower Barden*. The last firm were in financial straits in 1857; in October of that year their unpaid and unfed workers nearly created a riot in Skipton. The job at *Lower Barden* was finished in 1860 and the aqueducts to *Heaton* service reservoir were then commissioned fully. *Grimwith* was later the subject of complaints by the millowners who used its waters; eventually, in March 1893, its enlargement by raising the embankment was entrusted to J & M Hawley at a contract price of £10,697.

Hawleys presumably employed on this job the 3ft gauge locomotive which they acquired new in 1893, namely –

FLYING ROCKET   0-4-0 Wing (inverted saddle) tank, cyls. 8in x 12in
by W G Bagnall 1423 of 1893 – new 7/1893
At 20/5/1896, J & M Hawley (then of Nelson) advertised 'on completion of contract, Grimwith reservoir, one nearly new 3ft gauge 0-4-0 tank loco, 8in cyls, by Bagnall', which reconciles with the above. It is improbable that they used it on an ensuing Bolton Corporation drainage contract and by 1897 it is believed to have become THE DUKE in service of John Best & Sons, on Edinburgh's aqueduct from Talla.

Associated with other major works by the Yorkshire Water Authority's western division – successors to Bradford Water Department – has been the enlargement of *Grimwith*'s capacity just over seven-fold. A new earthfill embankment, with clay core, buries and embraces the original embankment of the 1860s (as raised by Hawleys in the 1890s), the new works being commenced in 1975–76, with completion in 1983–84. It is interesting that both 'fill' material to form the new bank and suitable clay for its core have been found immediately westward of the old reservoir and a stone quarry area to its south east. These findings imply that Hawleys' small locomotive would not have far to go to secure such materials, in 1893–96.

West of Bradford, *Stubden* and *Doe Park* reservoirs were constructed. At *Stubden*, owing to defects developing, a major reconstruction was in hand by 1876 but the contractors, Clapham Brothers, were lethargic. *Doe Park* reservoir (at Denholme) was threatened in November 1880 as the Great Northern Railway's Keighley branch line (engineer: Mr Fraser) was planned to intercept a flow of spring water which fed into it.

Projects initiated 1864–75 – by Charles Gott, engineer, of Bradford

Reconstruction of *Lower Barden* was completed circa 1874. *Horton Bank* and *Brayshaw* reservoirs, both local to Bradford, were built under Act of 1868 and largely completed by September 1877.

Compensation reservoirs at *Leeming* and *Leeshaw*, both near Oxenhope, were authorised by Act of 1869, built by Crabtree Brothers & Robert Sugden and both completed circa November 1878.

Brownroyd reservoir – to the west – was completed in February 1875, replacing older works taken over by the Bradford & Thornton Railway (G.N.R.).

Projects 1875–90 – by Alexander R Binnie, engineer

Upper Barden figured in this period and is discussed further below.

Thornton Moor, with filter beds, was the subject of Acts of 1873 and 1878 and a contract of September 1879 with Crabtree Brothers, of Oxenhope; completion was in 1885.

In February 1890, Crabtree Brothers, Oxenhope, offered for sale 'two 3ft gauge locomotives'. These could have been used on the Thornton Moor works of 1879–85 and may have played some part in constructing the earlier Leeming and Leeshaw reservoirs, c. 1870–78. Subsequently, Crabtrees were at Ramsden Clough (for Todmorden) in 1885–88; they offered 'a locomotive' from that site in 10/1888. There has also been a suggestion that Crabtrees owned VICTORIA (Bagnall 902 of 1887) at some time prior to its being Arnolds' BURN at Leighton, but most of its intermediate years are accounted for.

The contract for *Idle Hill* service reservoir was placed in March 1879 with Thomas Whiteley (Executors of T Whiteley by 6/1880; James T Whiteley by 9/1880). Completion was in 1880.

Gilstead filtration works, near Bingley in the Aire valley, were put in hand 1884–85, clearly by direct labour. Materials were carted from Bingley station. In June 1885 Mr Binnie authorised purchase of an engine for the works from Mr Anderton of Skipton for £77 and also the purchase of a horse – the engine being for stationary use?

Doe Park reservoir, here seen, was constructed for Bradford around 1860. In 1880, it was threatened as the impending construction of the Great Northern Railway's branch line to Keighley seemed likely to intercept an incoming flow of spring water. The view (circa 1910?), at Denholme station, is north eastward over the G.N.R. and reservoir, the dam hidden on the far left arm.

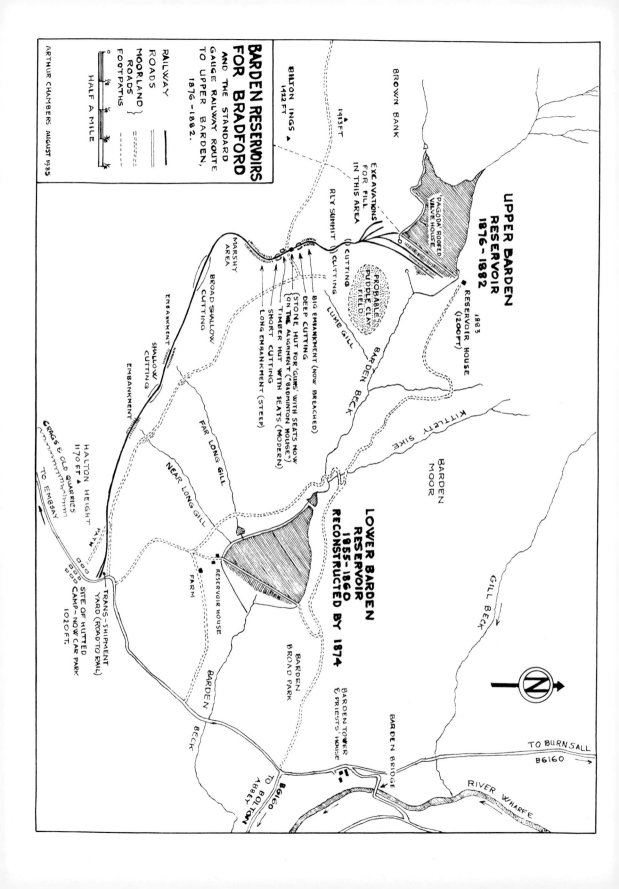

Chapter Eight

Upper Barden Reservoir

This was authorised by Act of 1875, as an impounding reservoir in the valley of the Barden beck, upstream of the then existing *Lower Barden* reservoir. Purchase of lands from the Barden Moor estate of the Duke of Devonshire was negotiated with the Duke's agent, Mr Wynne Jardine, whose estate office was at Chesterfield. The plans and specifications were the work of Alexander Binnie, waterworks engineer of Bradford Corporation, and in August 1876 a contract was placed conditionally with Mr Easton Gibb. A deputation from Bradford speedily visited Dundee and Aberdeen and satisfied themselves of Gibb's capabilities; he had built *Clatto* reservoir for Dundee, 1874, and earlier (in the 1850s?) built a reservoir for Aberdeen. His tender of £199,905.10.10d for *Upper Barden* was formally accepted 1 September 1876 and work soon went ahead. In May 1877, Easton Gibb was required to dismiss his manager from *Upper Barden* on account of persistent refusal to adhere to the specification. Subsequently, the name of W Gibb appears, on behalf of Easton Gibb, being by implication the partner appointed to take charge at site. From March 1878, George N Yourdi was resident engineer for the Corporation – and in later years he figured in projects having much railway interest as resident superintendent in Baldersdale (for Middlesbrough and Stockton) and also in the Elan valley (for Birmingham).

The site at Upper Barden is remote and the reservoir house, above the embankment's north east end and dated 1883, is just about on the 1200 ft contour, on the edge of Barden moor.

'Fill' for the earth embankment seems to have come mainly from an area south west of the bank site, judging by the appearance of the terrain today, and puddle clay is reputed to have been dug out of the valley bottom a little south of the 'fill' area and southward of the beck. Imports must have been hauled laboriously to the Halton Moor vantage point at 1020ft o.d. on the hilly byroad which climbs from Embsay and Eastby and drops away to Barden Scale. The carparking area here, popular with summer motorists today, is believed to be the site of Easton Gibb's hutted village for workers. Within a stonesthrow, one can set off to tramp northwards on a well-defined track which, from its earthworks, is demonstrably the course of the contractor's standard gauge railway, climbing up into the moorlands. Nearly two miles from the start of this route, beyond a stone shelter for the use of the 'guns', a deep cutting is followed by a major embankment, now badly eroded, at about the 1328ft spot point on the o.s. map. The bridleway thence swings westward, climbing to 1413ft, but it may be assumed that the railway dropped on a northerly course to reach the south end of the dam embankment; this last section of its route is lost in excavations, probably for 'fill'.

The navvies would enjoy a spectacular trip morning and evening on the 'paddy mail', which assuredly would be provided for them. Works included the tapping of Lumb gill (near the 1328ft point) and, well north of the embankment, Gill beck; also the making of by-channels and waste water courses and some tunnelling work. The making of the Gill beck conduit was by direct labour under James Johnson, who was the Corporation's superintendent resident at *Lower Barden*, and the Corporation paid for the keep of his horse in order that he might exercise supervision out on the moor.

Three standard gauge six-coupled locomotives were delivered new by Hunslet Engine Company of Leeds to Easton Gibb for this project, in 1879–80. As 'three 6-coupled tank engines by Hunslet' were offered for sale at Skipton station, 5 April 1883, on conclusion of the job, it may be deduced that they were the same ones and represented the complete locomotive stock. The location of the sale also suggests that in course of the job coal and other imports would come via Skipton station.

By May 1879, the cut-off trench along the foundation line of the embankment had evidently been excavated to the satisfaction of Alexander Binnie and it is on record that 'the filling of the main trench with concrete is about to commence'. Much attention was given then and subsequently to the method of filling, use of concrete for this purpose being exceptional at the time. In 1882 reference was made to 'the concrete trench and puddle wall', so presumably concrete was placed in the trench below ground level and puddle-clay was used in the embankment's central core above ground level. The steam locomotives would come into their own in handling cement to the site and may have played some part in haulage of 'fill' (and clay?) in the vicinity of the bank, but they were comparatively heavy and powerful for use on the embankment at so early a date, a time when engineers still relied upon dobbin carts for placing fill.

The valves were closed on 27 September 1882 and impounding commenced, the reservoir being full on 25 December 1882: capacity 429 million gallons. The embankment was 1573ft long and 125ft maximum height and at the time was adjudged 'the highest ever constructed in this country', notwithstanding a site rightly styled 'difficult and inaccessible'. Easton Gibb's work gave satisfaction. Years later, Easton Gibb & Son Limited made their name in waterside civil engineering at Newport and above all in creating the vast Rosyth naval base. Their managing director, Alexander Gibb, was appointed at the close of 1916 to the staff of the redoubtable General Sir Eric Geddes, Director General of Transport. Subsequently, Sir Alexander Gibb moved to engineering consultancy.

A vertical boiler locomotive by Alexander Chaplin & Company, their 371 of 1864, passed through the hands of at least two firms in Scotland before 10/1876, when it was with Easton Gibb & Company at Skipton. One may hazard that it worked in sidings at Skipton for a time, probably concerned with supplies imported by rail (or canal). However, it is understood to have been back with other owners in Scotland by 2/1877, so perhaps Easton Gibb found another locomotive or arranged for shunting by crane or by the Midland Railway.

Locomotives, standard gauge, of Easton Gibb at Upper Barden

JINGO
0-6-0 Saddle tank ic 13in x 18in 3ft 1in wheels
by Hunslet Engine Company 224 of 1879 – came new ex-works 24/4/1879 to Barden. The specification shows allowance of lateral movement in the trailing axleboxes, also compensating beams from leading to driving and driving to trailing springs (and these are seen in the photograph of the locomotive). Loco turned out green, lined and varnished with the name painted in shaded letters.
Sold in 4/1883 to Lucas & Aird, Hull, in time for their contracts building the Hull & Barnsley Railway and dock.
Later: with J T Firbank, as RICKMANSWORTH, doubtless on railway construction into 'Metroland', e.g. Rickmansworth–Chalfont–Chesham in late 1880s.

BRUCE
0-6-0 Saddle tank ic 14in x 18in 3ft 1in wheels
by Hunslet Engine Company 234 of 1880 – came new ex-works 26/2/1880 to Barden.
Sold to Kirk & Randall for construction work on the first major dock at Tilbury, the contract (with use of locos until completion 1886) being transferred to Lucas & Aird – carrying the name BRUCE on the contract but taken over by East & West India Dock Company and from 1889 London & India Docks Jt. Committee, with name MOTH.

WALLACE
0-6-0 Saddle tank ic 14in x 18in 3ft 1in wheels
by Hunslet Engine Company 235 of 1880 – came new ex-works 26/2/1880 to Barden.
Sold to Kirk & Randall for their Tilbury dock contract, completed by Lucas & Aird in 1886; passing like the previous loco to E & W India Dock Company and from 1889 London & India Docks Jt. Committee, with name BEE; and becoming Port of London Authority No. 25 in 1909 and being sold for scrap from West India Dock in 1913.

The name JINGO of 1879 is explained by the music hall refrain –

> We don't want to fight, but, by Jingo, if we do
> We've got the ships, we've got the men, and got the money too;

which had echoed the loudly proclaimed views of the anti-Czar party in Britain during the Russo-Turkish war of 1877–78. Swift had earlier made known the exclamation 'Hey, Jingo!'. Earlier again, it seems to have been imported with mercenaries from the Basque country.

In the Journal of the Industrial Locomotive Society, 1955, Mr G J Groves held that HE234/1880 was WALLACE, becoming No. 6 MOTH, and that HE235/1880 was BRUCE, becoming No. 2 BEE. The discrepancy relates to the names pre-1886 and I favour the version recorded in the maker's records and reproduced in my table.

Locomotive JINGO, standard gauge, is seen as turned out by Hunslet in 1879 to work for Easton Gibb on Upper Barden reservoir project, with daily climbs over a summit point above 1300ft o.d.

James Watson on the reservoirs and aqueducts

A paper and diagram of 6 September 1900 were presented by James Watson, then waterworks engineer to the city of Bradford; the summary already given of the earlier works for Bradford owes much to Mr Watson's paper and to that presented much later by Mr George Renton, waterworks engineer to the city. These presentations looked especially to the then current and prospective schemes in the valley of the Nidd.

Chapter Nine

Railways and Reservoirs in the Upper Valley of the Nidd

Introduction to the Nidd valley

The North Eastern Railway's branch line from Ripley Junction, a little north of Harrogate, up Nidderdale to Pateley Bridge opened on 1 May 1862, conveying passengers and goods. The passenger service, Harrogate to Pateley Bridge, ceased from 2 April 1951 and goods traffic from 2 November 1964, the branch being lifted in the first half of 1965.

A link, N.E.R. owned, beyond Pateley Bridge station, enabled stone to be brought from sidings at the foot of the private incline, which came down from Scotgate Ash quarries, located in the hillside immediately north east of the town. These quarries of Scotgate Ash Stone Company Limited (incorporated 1872) ceased production in about 1914. The quarries are believed to have belonged circa 1860 to the Metcalfe family, who had other local interests too, and to have provided one of the reasons for promotion of the N.E.R. line. It is on record that the incline from the quarries down to the N.E.R. (with wire rope and drum) was under construction in June 1871, with J G Metcalfe, the then owner of Scot Gate Ash Stone Company, as promoter.

Pateley Bridge N.E.R. station and the link to the quarry incline foot sidings provided access to an exceptionally varied and interesting group of twentieth century lines, which reached out through the more sylvan portion of the upper dale to the remote and wild country where the Nidd and Stone beck rise at about 2000ft close below the ridge of Great Whernside and, in a couple of miles, flow into Angram reservoir. Angram is superb in its remoteness on a still midsummer day. It is inspiring on a January day, when at times the north-westerly gale funnels down so fiercely that one cannot struggle into it, and the overflowing waters cascade over the dam wall in magnificent falls; sheets of spray are carried by the wind clear over a walker on the service roadway which is supported on a colonnade of arches above the crest of the dam. It was to build this reservoir, and Scar House reservoir below it, that men, railways and steam power came to upper Nidderdale.

Bradford Corporation's Nidd Valley scheme in outline

The story goes back to 1887–88 when the Corporation of Bradford discovered that Leeds Corporation had laid claim to the valley of the river Burn above Masham. Alexander Binnie, still waterworks engineer to the city of Bradford at that time, concentrated his own investigations upon the upper valley of the Nidd and the means of impounding waters there and bringing them to Bradford. From correspondence published in July 1889 by John Hardaker (*Bradford Water Supply – Remarks on the Grimwith and Nidd Schemes*), we know that during Christmas week 1887, Alexander Binnie and Professor A H Green, F.R.S., geologist, of Oxford spent three days together investigating the geology of the upper Nidd valley at a somewhat preliminary stage of Binnie's scheme. The Professor saw no geological problem at the proposed sites of dams, which he described as Angram and Haden Carr. The scheme, as brought to an essentially final form, provided for reservoirs at *Angram, Haden Carr, Woodale* and *Gouthwaite* – in this order down the dale, *Gouthwaite* being a compensation reservoir to maintain supplies to those holding rights to water from the Nidd. A Bill was submitted to Parliament and became the Bradford Corporation Water Act 1890 (Assent 14 August 1890). However, in February 1890, Alexander Binnie left Bradford to become chief engineer to the London County Council.

James Watson, from Dundee (with experience of waterworks construction as chief there), was appointed waterworks engineer, Bradford, in December 1890. He was responsible for adjustments to the overall scheme and the Act of 1890 was amended in some respects by the Bradford Corporation Water Act 1892 (Assent 27 June 1892). The three upper reservoirs, not greatly changed, emerged as –

Angram at 1187.5ft o.d., to hold 810 million gallons (in the event its capacity was 1100 million gallons).
Haden Carr (the alternative title of 'Lodge' was not adopted) at 1098ft o.d., to hold 1088 million gallons.
High Woodale at 994ft o.d., to hold 698 million gallons.

The heights quoted are proposed top water level above ordnance datum. *High Woodale* was never built but *Scar House* took its place much later and absorbed *Haden Carr*, which had been formed in the interim.

A main aqueduct, 32 miles in its 1892 form, branch aqueducts and other works were provided for, in order to carry the impounded waters to Bradford.

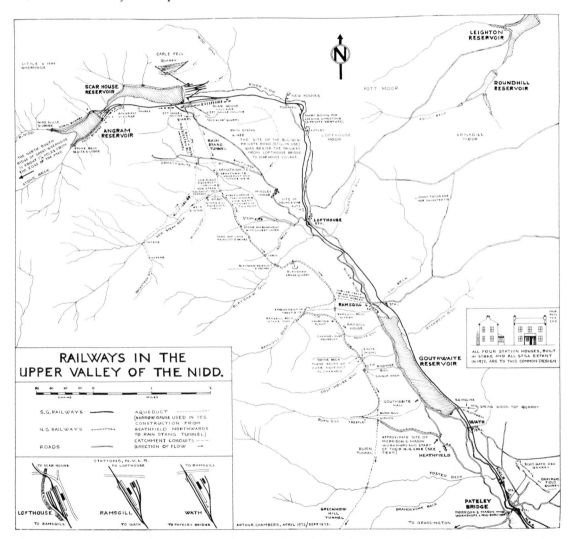

This map (necessarily much reduced in size) is reproduced here in its entirety so that readers can appreciate, at a glance, the complete geography of the area and the full extent of the various railways. Detail enlargements will be found later in the narrative.

Aqueduct construction in upper Nidderdale
by Morrison & Mason Limited, of Glasgow

A scene believed to be at the south end (Skyreholme) of 6200 yds long Greenhow Hill tunnel. The rail gauge is probably less than the 3ft employed north of this tunnel and it is not known that locomotives were employed in or immediately south of the tunnel.

Loading 42in diameter pipes for the aqueduct.

Chapter Ten

Haden Carr Dam and the Aqueduct to Bradford – Morrison and Mason Ltd.

The dam to create Haden Carr reservoir was built under contract to the Corporation by Morrison and Mason Limited, of Glasgow, in the 'nineties. It was a masonry dam and a photograph taken 4 October 1899 shows it essentially complete and the lake overflowing. The dam does not appear particularly high and there are railway tracks (gauge?) on the plateau below its face and a tip wagon but neither locomotives nor horses appear. I have been assured that horses, not locomotives, were employed.

Morrison and Mason also built, under contract then valued at £286,259.7.10d, the original aqueduct comprising a single line of pipes from Haden Carr to *Chellow Heights*, a new service reservoir on the approaches to Bradford, and they used steam locomotives on at least one section of this work. The route comprised –

14⅜ miles of pipes (presumably on the surface of the ground).
11½ miles of 'cut and cover' work (including most of the portion between Rain Stang and Burn
    tunnels and the first three miles south of Greenhow Hill tunnel).
6⅛ miles of tunnels.

These tunnels, from north to south, were –

Rain Stang	2,421 yards: headings met 8 February 1899
Burn	1,884 yards: headings met 8 October 1899
Greenhow Hill	6,204 yards: work embraced circa 1894–99 (and on completion in October 1899 the Corporation granted £5 towards the expenses of the workmen's celebration).
North End	374 yards

The job also included branch aqueducts totalling about 5¾ miles and dams, intakes, weirs, bridge and chambers.

The aqueduct passed under the Skipton–Ilkley railway near Bolton Abbey and bridged the Midland 'main line' near Bingley. All the aqueduct works were embraced by 'Contract No. 2' of December 1893 and the work continued until completion in 1901. Morrison and Mason had a construction yard at Heathfield, with blacksmith's shop, etc., and locomotive shed.

The contractor's narrow gauge railway ran from near the barn on the gated road at the north end of Heathfield village over the moors in a generally north westerly direction, bridging the Burn gill and following the cut-and-cover of the aqueduct to Raygill House and over Ramsgill beck to above Lofthouse and onwards to the syphon chamber on the south bank of How Stean beck. There is no evidence that the line negotiated the deep ravine of How Stean nor the closely ensuing crossings of Low Riggs and Armathwaite gills to the exit from Rain Stang tunnel. The gauge of this exciting railway has been variously recalled as 2ft, 2ft 6in and 3ft. Deductions are possible from knowledge of the light railway equipment which Morrison and Mason had employed elsewhere in the immediately preceding years, also from locomotives which are identified as working for M & M on their contracts for Bradford. They completed Thirlmere dam in the Lake District, for Manchester Corporation, in 1894, likewise tunnelling and aqueduct works on the same project; their railway material on those jobs is believed by the writer to have been lighter than would be required for steam traction. M & M had also been engaged constructing Craigmaddie reservoir, at Milngavie, for Glasgow Corporation; that work was commenced in 1888 and by 1889 three locomotives were in use – two believed on 3ft gauge and one on 2ft gauge, that last mentioned being graced by the staff with the title of 'The Mugdock

Hen'. Memories were of three locomotives on the slopes of Upper Nidderdale. There were at least two drivers. One was Jim Chadwick, who had come from work at Thirlmere. Another was Kit Armstrong, who lived in Lofthouse during the job and whose engine was in course of time stabled near Raygill House. Chinny Young has also been quoted as a driver but is alternatively remembered as a rope runner with the locos (Dan Young, his father, was a foreman with M & M). The two locomotives which it has been possible to list were both of 3ft gauge so we may take it that the line described, from Heathfield northwards, was on that gauge, with the possibility that a narrower gauge was used for access to the tunnels.

It is not certain whether the contractors in fact used railways extensively south of Heathfield but temporary tracks (gauge not clear) figure in a photograph of the aqueduct bridge over the Wharfe at Barden Tower near Bolton Abbey. Use of horses and carts on the aqueduct has been recalled.

Morrison and Mason had their headquarters at Pateley Bridge during the time of their works in Nidderdale. Workshops and huts were in the area west of the river, where a garage stands today. Most of the men and horses had come from Thirlmere and many went on with the firm to the Elan valley pipeline construction after the Bradford pipeline had been completed. It will be observed (below) that locomotives went on there in the late 'nineties.

At Riddings Gill bridge, built to carry the aqueduct from, initially, Angram reservoir; the view is on 2 March 1895, with a 3ft gauge locomotive by Andrew Barclay, lettered MORRISON & MASON Ltd. A probable principal of the contractors stands, kilted, on the railway line.

Locomotives, 3ft gauge, of Morrison and Mason, believed on the aqueduct

0-4-0 Side tank oc 6in dia and wheels 1ft 10in
   by Andrew Barclay 746 of circa 1894 – new to M & M. If at Craigmaddie, this was not for long; a spares order for brake blocks from Craigmaddie 11/8/1894 may have been for this loco but by 3/1895 spares for it were ordered from 'Bradford' and from 8/1895 until 4/1898 from Pateley Bridge. It went next with M & M to the Birmingham pipeline (spares required at Knighton by 7/1898). The loco had a varied career with M & M, Arrols and John Best.

0-4-0 Side tank oc 6in dia and wheels 1ft 10in
   by Andrew Barclay 761 of circa 1895 – new to M & M at 'Bradford'; spares to Pateley 8/1895 and 4/1898. On Birmingham job by 12/1898 and had a long career with M & M and other owners.

Heading northward from Riddings Gill bridge, the aqueduct had to cross Ramsgill ravine not by a viaduct but by syphon ('down and up again'). Here is the spectacular scene when the constructional railway made the crossing – the view believed to be southward. Alderman Gadie is the the right, maybe the then chairman of the waterworks committee to the left.

An intake dam (foreground) has been built on Ramsgill Beck. The view is downstream towards the syphon and Nidderdale. The narrow gauge 'main route' for loco haulage is visible heading back towards Heathfield (and Greenhow tunnel). Also discernible is its northward divergence crossing the Beck (straight ahead) by a trestle bridge.

A special occasion on the aqueduct line: one of the 3ft gauge Barclay 'pugs' poses, heading north towards Blayshaw Gill viaduct.

Hardgap Lane viaduct for the aqueduct – and temporarily for the substantial 3ft gauge railway – is being built: again, a Barclay 'pug' poses. The date is 20 May 1897.

Northward again, Morrison & Mason's 3ft gauge line probably ended at a syphon house near the camera. In this view of 8 September 1973 the aqueduct pipebridge of the 1890s, still very much in use, is seen on the right. Edale Construction are building a bridge (and syphon) for an additional line of pipes and using light track to permit lowering of the pipe lengths to position. This crossing, essentially by syphon, is of How Stean Beck. Ahead, two more bridges cross tributary streams to reach the Rain Stang 2420 yds tunnel near Armathwaite farm. The intake from Angram and Scar House reservoirs is just beyond the tunnel.

Chapter Eleven

Chellow Heights Reservoirs – Phineas Drake, Contractor

The Act of 1890 provided for the aqueduct to convey the Nidd waters to the existing service reservoir at Heaton, in Bradford's northern suburbs. From there, water would have to be pumped to the (extensive) higher districts; this would involve installing and maintaining expensive pumping plant.

In his first year as waterworks engineer, James Watson reviewed the whole vast project and, in September 1891, he proposed that two new service reservoirs be constructed at Chellow Heights, strategically sited at about 800ft o.d. on the ridge between the Aire valley and the city of Bradford and that the new main aqueduct from Nidderdale should terminate at Chellow Heights, thus obviating the need for pumping plant. These were the main changes in the Act of 1892. Lands at Chellow Heights were bought from Mr J A Jowett and permanent access route easements negotiated with the agent for the Earl of Rosse. The contract went in September 1895 to Phineas Drake, of Bradford, whose sureties for performance were James Drake, of Manningham, 'gentleman', and John Drake, also of Manningham but described as 'contractor'. The works, twin reservoirs of 64 million gallons combined capacity and 10 filter beds, were tackled at once and completed in 1900, when Phineas Drake also built the reservoir keeper's house. The construction involved walls round all sides made of masonry and concrete, with facing to the water of large selected stones, laid in cement mortar and backed by high quality concrete, with clay puddle outside that again. These totally artificial reservoirs were to be floored in concrete 14in thick, with clay puddle 14–18in thick beneath it.

Photographs of 1898–99 show the handsome masonry valve tower dated 1897, with the city's arms. There is a contractor's shed at a little distance, outside the water area, and wooden tip wagons on track which may be standard gauge at the filters. Probably rail mounted cranes and horses sufficed for motive power. It is known that Drake tendered in October 1902 for Bury's Ogden reservoir (Haslingden Grane) but did not secure that contract until its negotiated transfer by Fosters of Bradford in June 1905; his firm then promptly took over Fosters' 3ft gauge locomotives and acquired two more but there is no suggestion that they had hitherto been locomotive owners.

Chellow Grange and lands abutting on Chellow Heights reservoirs were leased by Bradford Corporation in 1900 for conversion to a golf course.

Chapter Twelve

Gouthwaite Reservoir – John Best & Son, Edinburgh

Concurrent with Morrison and Mason's contracts was the first one taken on in Nidderdale by another Scots firm, John Best and Son, whose work we encounter elsewhere. Gouthwaite compensation reservoir was formed by Best, who built the dam just above Wath to impound 1610 million gallons of water, stretching two miles, right up to Ramsgill churchyard. The contract was placed in June 1893 with 'Mr John Best' and the first sod was cut by James Watson, at the dam site on 13 September 1893. Best's first job was to make a new channel to the west of the site to divert the river Nidd. Gouthwaite Hall and several farms were demolished. A quarry was developed at Spring Wood Top, some 500 yards from the dam and up on the east side of the valley; a railway incline, standard gauge, brought the stone down to the dam and it is confirmed by a photograph that the line crossed the top of the dam as it came to completion – but there was no access line over the two miles from Pateley Bridge and horses, not locomotives, worked on the construction site. The dam wall was formed of earth at the west end but the major part was of masonry rubble, set in cement, with large blocks of hard gritstone on the face and back, bedded and jointed in cement mortar. The overflow passes over the top of the dam, surmounted by a carriage road on fourteen arches. Some six years after commencement, in October 1899, the reservoir was allowed to fill and owing to abnormal rain it did so in three days and overflowed prematurely: it is reported that the contractor's huts, plant and cement sheds floated derelict on the waters. Final completion was in 1901, after eight years work, at a cost of £240,000 to the Corporation, to be compared with an original contract price of £118,551 in June 1893.

'The Alderman's Rest' was the lighthearted title for Gouthwaite Lodge, seen in this up-dale view from the valley road, Pateley Bridge to Lofthouse. John Best & Son built the dam – just off the picture to the right – and associated works during 1893–1901. The course of the subsequent railway, first on 3ft gauge, then for years on standard gauge, was along the easterly shore, glimpsed across the water if looking to the right of the building.

Chapter Thirteen

Forward to Angram, 1900–1904

The Bradford Corporation's Water Department was now, in 1900–1901, looking ahead to the construction of Angram dam, high up the valley, under the parliamentary authority of 1892. In September 1901 they decided to proceed with plans and sections for Angram embankment (at a location differing from that shown in earlier parliamentary plans) and for a road to it, also it was proposed to invite tenders for the execution of the work. Meanwhile, current and promised activity in the upper dale attracted interest from as far away as London. Power & Traction Ltd of Westminster was a company with Yorkshire associations, having on their board Mr Greenwood of Greenwood & Batley Ltd, Leeds, whose firm (part of Hunslet Engine Company since December 1980) have been manufacturers of electric vehicles from early days and supplied equipment to electric tramways. The London company applied for powers under the Light Railways Act 1896 to construct a light railway from Pateley Bridge to Lofthouse, passing along the east bank of Gouthwaite reservoir. The Light Railway Commissioners held an enquiry at Harrogate on 9 October 1900. The N.V.L.R. Order 1901 in favour of Power & Traction Ltd resulted, the railway to be to a gauge of 2ft 6in. The Bradford Corporation had kept in touch with this project and in August 1902 the promoters were negotiating with the Corporation for an easement in and through land adjoining Gouthwaite reservoir. In January 1903 the Corporation agreed to invest up to £2,000 in shares in the Light Railway. In June the Corporation sub-committee was still in favour of the investment but the matter was further investigated. The Corporation engineer, Mr Watson, met Henry Jackson, the contractor proposed by the Company, and in the same month a strong deputation was formed to interview the Company and contractor in London. A subsequent minute implies that the Company was not prepared to go ahead with their project, and in July the Corporation rescinded their decision to subscribe. At the same time they agreed to invite tenders for Angram and the following month provisional agreement was reached with the Nidd Valley Light Railway Company and Power & Traction Ltd (its proprietors) for the Corporation to purchase the powers under the N.V.L.R. Order to construct the Light Railway. Considerable debate upon the gauge of the Light Railway thereupon ensued. The Light Railway Commissioners' authority to alter the gauge from 2ft 6in to 3ft was to be sought and enough land was to be bought 'to enable a full gauge light railway to be constructed at any future time.' Probably John Best advised adopting 3ft gauge in view of his knowledge that contractors' rolling stock was available in this gauge. The North Eastern Railway were by now taking a keen interest and repeatedly urged that the Light Railway gauge should be 4ft 8½in. Mr P Burtt, traffic superintendent, pointed out in July 1904 that the N.E.R. were running excursions to Pateley Bridge twice weekly and that standard gauge would permit these passenger trains running through over the N.V.L.R. and it would avoid transfer of goods.

The Board of Trade were reluctant to establish the precedent of a Municipal Corporation constructing a Light Railway outside its own area when not in continuation of an existing tramway or light railway from the boundary of its district! Nevertheless they screwed up their courage to give formal approval on 30 December 1903 and the Bradford Corporation (Nidd Valley Transfer) Light Railway Order 1904 (1 March) resulted. Borrowing not exceeding £30,000 was authorised in the Order and an Amendment Order 1908 increased these borrowing powers to £66,000, over the signature of Winston S Churchill, President of the Board of Trade. The B.O.T. had agreed to the alternative of standard gauge in May 1904 and construction to this gauge increased the eventual costs.

Interesting light is thrown on interim plans at this period by a layout diagram dated 21 March 1904 prepared by the district engineer, N.E.R., York. This shows the proposed terminal arrangements in Pateley Bridge for a passenger carrying railway using narrow gauge. There was already in existence a standard gauge level crossing from the N.E.R. station goods yard over the road and onwards to the incline foot, then up the incline to Scotgate Ash quarries. The narrow gauge line is shown starting immediately north of the level crossing, between the standard gauge one and the river. A single platform, 93 yards long, with railway offices, appears on the left (west) side and there is a loop on leaving the station. It is implied that exchange facilities for goods from the standard gauge to this narrow gauge line are provided in a 'contractor's yard' (not within the scope of the plan) a little further north, probably about where the eventual Nidd Valley Light Railway had its locomotive and carriage sheds.

In October–November 1903 John Best's tender of £365,492 for Angram was accepted, and contracts were placed for associated works remote from the dale –

Hartshead reservoir	–	£6,784.7.7d with H Arnold & Son
Pudsey reservoir	–	£6,543 with P Drake
Calverley Moor reservoir	–	£6,706.16.3d with Jeptha Thornton & Son

John Scott of Darlington, whom one meets in connection with Teesdale railways and reservoirs, withdrew a tender for light railways in the Nidd valley and, also in October–November 1903, John Best's tenders were accepted for –

1. the N.V.L.R., Pateley Bridge to Lofthouse – £20,300 (subject to the transfer powers being forthcoming from the B.O.T.)
2. A 'Tramway' from Lofthouse to Angram reservoir – £5,385

A road to Angram: Holme & King Ltd

Early in April 1902 the tender of Holme & King Ltd, of Liverpool, for building a private road from the public road at Lofthouse to Angram dam site was accepted: £20,451.8.2d. By mid-August 1902 a progress payment was authorised, so presumably the work was in hand. When the Corporation negotiated purchase of land for this road, they had reserved the right to make a Tramway or Light Railway along one side of the road. Until the road was built there was a ford just beyond Lofthouse.

It has been suggested that Holme & King built the 3ft gauge contractor's railway ('tramway') beside the road, although the original contract for this was with Best, who was quite capable of building access railways to his sites. However this may be, the two probably overlapped and Holme & King used at least two 3ft gauge railway locomotives, namely –

XIT 0-4-0 Saddle tank oc 8in x 14in
by Manning Wardle 475 of 1873.
This little engine was described by the makers as 'an extensive alteration of M.W. ordinary class D to suit 3'0" gauge.'
Its original owners were Rosedale & Ferryhill Iron Company, with the name ROSEDALE carried and it worked at the Rosedale East ironstone mines, above Rosedale Abbey in Yorkshire. The Company suspended payment in 1879 and was wound up.
The locomotive soon reappeared, with the public works contractors S Pearson & Son, probably used by them in 1879 on main drainage works at Southport. It was engaged on their major contract for making the Blackwall tunnel under the Thames, a job of 1890–97. Probably before the tunnel was completed, XIT (now known as such) was engaged for Holme and King of Liverpool on reservoir works of 1896 onwards at Upper Neuadd in the Brecon mountains. Next probably came the preparatory muck-shifting (and quite an alteration to the local landscape) at Brighouse, part of an H & K contract with the Lancashire & Yorkshire Railway to widen a double track to four roads, job of 1899–1902. A sojourn at Prescot, near Liverpool, where H & K secured a contract in 10/1900 to make Prescot reservoir for Liverpool waterworks, was apparently fitted in, but XIT was stated in Nidderdale to have come, doubtless in spring 1902, from Brighouse to the dale.

The loco is delightfully illustrated in use at Lofthouse and also appears to figure on the ceremonial train of 7/1904.

After Nidderdale days, XIT remained with H & K and in due course was employed by them on contracts around Coventry, notably the building of Courtaulds' factory (probably strictly on the site preparation) and new railway construction from Three Spires Junction (on the Nuneaton–Coventry line) out south-eastward to join the London line: known as the Coventry Loop line of the London & North Western Railway. H & K went into liquidation in 1913; the contract passed to J Wilson & Sons but H & K's plant would become L&NWR property, hence XIT was offered for sale on behalf of the L&NWR at Gosford Green (on the Loop) on 23/7/1914. Soon after the war started, XIT joined Underwood and Brother(s), of Dukinfield, on their Penderyn reservoir works near Aberdare. Underwoods and their successors the Mountain Ash U.D.C. were at work there until c. 1920 but XIT was believed to have left site earlier. A hint may be an advertisement of 11/6/1919 by the Ministry of Munitions, at Darlington: it mentioned locomotive 'X'. One might think this was the end but in 5/1927 Hunslets as successors to the makers supplied for Manning Wardle 475 of 1873, namely XIT, new wheels, axles and crankpins – but frustratingly it is not now on record to whom or whither they went.

The name XIT on neat plates on the saddle tank sides was in block letters but with an initial capital 'X' and smaller 'IT'. Many is the time I have asked old hands who well remembered this little engine, what did this mean? Always the response was 'Exit'! – but that was no satisfying solution. Recently, Russell Wear, researcher and author, chanced on the fact that, in the sixteenth century, King Edward VI had a servant who was short of stature – and called Xit. As the little 'Manning' probably acquired its name in the Blackwall tunnel, an association is perceived.

XIT, by Manning Wardle of 1873, a much travelled little 3ft gauge locomotive, is seen at Lofthouse-in-Nidderdale as property of Holme & King Limited, who built the private road onwards up the dale from Lofthouse to Angram. The original of this print hints at the existence of standard gauge as well as 3ft gauge by this time.

NIDD 0-4-0 Saddle tank oc 8in x 12in
by W G Bagnall 1658 – new 7/1902 to Holme & King at Pateley Bridge and still with them in Nidderdale in 7/1907. It went to H Arnold & Son by 3/1909 for their work on Leighton reservoir in Colsterdale, being taken over the intervening moors by horse haulage, relieved in the latter part by Atkinson's traction engine; it was at Masham on 6/6/1926 before the final sale there, but would by then be property of Leeds Corporation.

Holme & King undertook dock construction at Garston for the L&NWR and L&YR, roughly contemporary with their work in Nidderdale, but employing standard gauge locomotives. They had Foden steam wagons, so it was recalled, used to bring materials from Pateley Bridge to Lofthouse.

NIDD, by W.G. Bagnall, 1902, poses outside the makers' works at Stafford, where observe the 'up' main line signals of the London & North Western Railway main line, the West Coast Main Line. This 3ft gauge locomotive proceeded from Stafford to join Holme & King at Lofthouse and engage in the road works. It figures again in our story as one of Harold Arnold's locomotives during his work on Leighton reservoir – 'over the hill' – circa 1909–1914.

On 13 July 1904, the first sod of the Nidd Valley Light Railway was cut near Gouthwaite dam and, later in the day, in the dale head, a ceremony at Angram dam site included presentation of this 15 in long silver model of a contractor's side tipping wagon. The City of Bradford arms and an engraved plaque figure. Many years later, the model came up for sale at Christies, in 1977.

The train which conveyed the party from Sykes Brow, just short of Lofthouse, right through to Angram site for the sod-cutting and presentation ran on 3ft gauge. The first locomotive will be XIT and it carries a brass plate inscribed 'Holme & King, Liverpool'. The second loco is ANGRAM (seen again subsequently), property of John Best & Son. Notable figures include: Adam Sloan, walking ganger for Bests' firm, in light suit and trilby hat, in front of ANGRAM; Sandy McCallum, Snr., on footplate of XIT, hand on brake; Herbert Clegg, timekeeper for H & K Ltd, to right of the bicycle; Allan Best, who took charge of Bests' work in Nidderdale, 1904–1917, in the main group on the ground; Bob Byrom, walking ganger for H & K Ltd is on XIT, centrally; and Mr Widenden, site agent for H & K Ltd, wearing breeches and leggings, on XIT.

Chapter Fourteen

Angram Reservoir – John Best & Son/John Best & Sons Ltd, 1903–1920

As mentioned previously, John Best & Son, who had already built Gouthwaite reservoir in the dale, secured the contract for Angram in November 1903. Holme & King had been making the private road and now Best got to work and established a base at Lofthouse in the area which became the station yard, necessarily bringing materials by the twisting valley road from the N.E.R. railhead at Pateley Bridge and, within eight months of obtaining the contract, had a 3ft gauge line laid down on the left (going up the valley) of the private road, Lofthouse to Angram, some 6½ miles of route. A bridge of 20ft span crossed the Nidd just beyond Lofthouse and the route onwards, beside the private road, was steep and winding. Best next set to work to extend this narrow gauge down the valley from Lofthouse to Pateley Bridge on the alignment over which he was to build the Corporation's Nidd Valley Light Railway.

The first red letter day in the contractor's calendar was Wednesday, 13 July 1904, when members of the Bradford City Council and their guests arrived at Pateley Bridge by special trains, a party numbering 150. They were conveyed in road carriages, first for a couple of miles to assemble on a slope near the north east corner of Gouthwaite dam; here the Lord Mayor of Bradford ceremonially cut the first sod for construction of the Nidd Valley Light Railway. After an hour here, the cavalcade of carriages continued up the shore of Gouthwaite reservoir, past Ramsgill village to the foot of Syke's brow, about a half mile short of Lofthouse. This would be the spot where the N.V.L.R. was to cross the road, on the level. Best's 3ft gauge line had been built southwards as far as this point (and it is on record that work on the line to Pateley Bridge had in fact been started at several points). A train of 'fifteen navvy wagons, fitted with seats and with two locomotives' was waiting, and the party enjoyed an hour's run in this train to Angram site where Mr John Best, principal of the contractors, made two presentations – to Alderman Holdsworth, a model railway wagon, 15in long, made in silver and on silver rails; to Alderman Milner (in his absence, as he was unwell), a model of a contractor's end-tipping wagon, in silver, on silver rails and with shields (carrying, presumably, the City arms). The models had been made by Fattorini & Sons, the well-known Bradford silversmiths. Alderman Holdsworth afterwards turned a sod on the line of the future dam, this being the main object of the pilgrimage. After refreshments, the outward route was retraced in due course, but without the deviation at Gouthwaite. A well-known picture of the train is reproduced, taken near the site of the (much later) tunnel. The locomotive nearest the camera is presumed to be XIT, Holme & King's Manning Wardle, built in 1873. The other locomotive is ANGRAM, by Hudswell Clarke 1892, property of John Best. It had only just arrived from Ireland, where I have had it recalled by a man who worked as a lad for Best on his Cork, Blackrock and Passage Railway project, completed 1904. Its Northumbrian name WHITTLE DEAN gave place to ANGRAM on coming to Nidderdale.

The narrow gauge was quickly pushed through to Pateley Bridge and ANGRAM was a main line locomotive ('route engine' in contract parlance) and BUNTY by Bagnall, fresh from being CROSSHAVEN on the Irish job, was stationed at Pateley Bridge and worked in the narrow gauge sidings there for perhaps two years, until displaced by standard gauge working and sent up to Angram site. Its original name was local to the C.B. & P.R., whilst BUNTY was a daughter of Best. An Andrew Barclay locomotive of 1887, TULLIBARDINE (after the Marquess of Tullibardine, Blair Castle, Blair Athol) also came from the C.B.P.R. contract and took the name EILEEN after another Best daughter, and this locomotive shared the working of the 'route' during the period of narrow gauge operation. Incidentally, some time was spent by me trying to trace an Eileen in Ireland, which seemed a likely quarter for such a lass – until discovering the facts of the matter.

The first standard gauge locomotive was towed from Pateley to Sykes Bank by a Foden steam wagon, driven by Mr Atkinson, a cousin of Arthur Atkinson of Masham fame (and Harrogate).

More informal is a Best owned 3ft gauge loco, by Hudswell Clarke 1892, fresh from Ireland as WHITTLE DEAN but by now named ANGRAM, with Mr McKay on the footplate. Attached is Best's saloon KITTY, with I suggest Allan Best on the step. The lad holds a sprag for dexterous, indeed hazardous, use in wagon wheels. The scene is believed to be in Pateley Yard (of Bests) in short-lived 3ft gauge days, indeed with an element of s.g. seen.

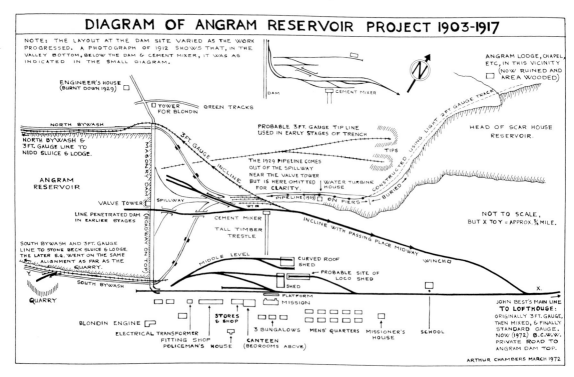

This remarkable cavalcade drove up the road, before the days of tarred surfaces, the railway engine's wheels cutting into the surface and the intrepid Atkinson ignoring the police sergeant's efforts to arrest his progress.

As standard gauge rails were put down both north and south of Lofthouse, the 'route' and sidings became mixed gauge; this has been recalled and is also apparent in one or two surviving photographs. The late William Kerr remembered that when he went to work at Angram around 1906, the 'three-legged rail' was in process of being pulled out, and by September 1907 the goods traffic had probably gone over to standard gauge for some time and the N.V.L.R. itself was fit for passenger trains – but more of this later.

To accommodate the workforce a 'temporary' village was built by Best during 1905. It was sited well up on the left hand side of the valley, mostly to the left of the road and railway as they approached the site of the dam. First came the school, built for the West Riding Education Authority, and there would be a house for Mr Shackleton, the schoolmaster; then the missioner's house; followed by the living huts for the workmen, found well built, warmed and ventilated when the Corporation's water sub-committee inspected the new village on 27 October 1905. The mission church, a single storey building with two gabled porches, had the short railway passenger platform in front of it and three superior bungalow residences (gabled) on the hill behind. The mission was followed immediately by the two storey canteen (with living quarters upstairs) prominent in photographs of the 'railway station', and a single storey continuation housed the grocer's and general stores, the latter managed by Mr John Storey of Pateley Bridge, whilst Mr Wigglesworth managed the canteen for Mr Best. The policeman had a detached bungalow on the slope up above the stores. Other worthies accommodated included the medical man, Doctor Holmes. There was a hospital and this was located on an isolated site above the line but before reaching the main village.

The accompanying plan, which seeks to reconstruct the layout at Angram at the height of the job, shows the village and also the 'industrial' buildings – fitting shop and other workshops above the line and the cement shed below, served by rail and feeding, via the tall timber trestle, the concrete mixer down on the valley floor far below. Some doubt surrounds the location of the locomotive shed and, by the time standard gauge arrived, there were two sheds on this side of the valley at Angram.

A diverging line descended a winch-operated incline of about 1 in 15 to the mixer and provided access to the dam foot and, in the early stages, penetration beyond it. A branch bridged the stream to sidings and another crossed to ascend a fierce three rail incline up the far side of the valley. This must have been to some extent self-acting as it incorporated a passing place for the wagons on the rope, but at the top was a steam winch with vertical boiler, which had initially been brought, with its coal, to its elevated site by the byways on the upper slopes of the dale, but which pulled all its coal up the incline thereafter and brought up stone for various purposes, including particularly a water channel up the valley – mentioned a little later. One building stood, isolated and remote, high on the far slope; this was the engineer's house or office and it remained until burnt down in 1929.

The building of the dam differed from most British waterworks as it was not to be an earth embankment with core of sealing clay, but was constructed of concrete pillars and huge rough hewn stones, the structure faced externally in handsome dressed stone. A 'blondin' (aerial ropeway) spanned the valley above the dam and the bucket was operated from a steam engine on the southerly hillside.

As the core of concrete and stone was laboriously built up during the years of construction, a temporary gantry carried rail tracks for flat stone-carrying wagons above the working area and derricks were rigged, using the wagons of stone to anchor their poles. There were isolated tracks, believed 3ft gauge, down in the valley floor near and parallel with the dam, and the 'blondin' sometimes lowered contractors' wagons loaded with such items as sacks of cement to these tracks, but locomotives were not employed there.

Best opened up a quarry on the hilltop nearly two miles further down the valley and above the (later) Scar village site. An incline descended from this quarry to join the main line and the

Around Angram site, construction era, 1904–1911

John Bests' s.g. 'pug' visibly lettered '7' (but '17' more probable), on the level of the main route, with buildings, left to right: accommodation for men; mission, with passenger platform in front; canteen, with quarters above; stores/shop.

With 'passenger train' above on the main level, here is the next level down, ladies picking their way to a point of vista.

On much the same level, a Barclay 'pug' of Bests is shunting onto the gantry staging to feed the requirements, notably cement, of the concrete mixer below. Beyond it, the ascending line from the valley bottom (below, left) to the main route (above, right) is seen, also a power house chimney in the valley.

The ascending line rises from the valley floor, the chimney relating to the previous view.

PATELEY BRIDGE EXCHANGE SIDINGS 1904-07.

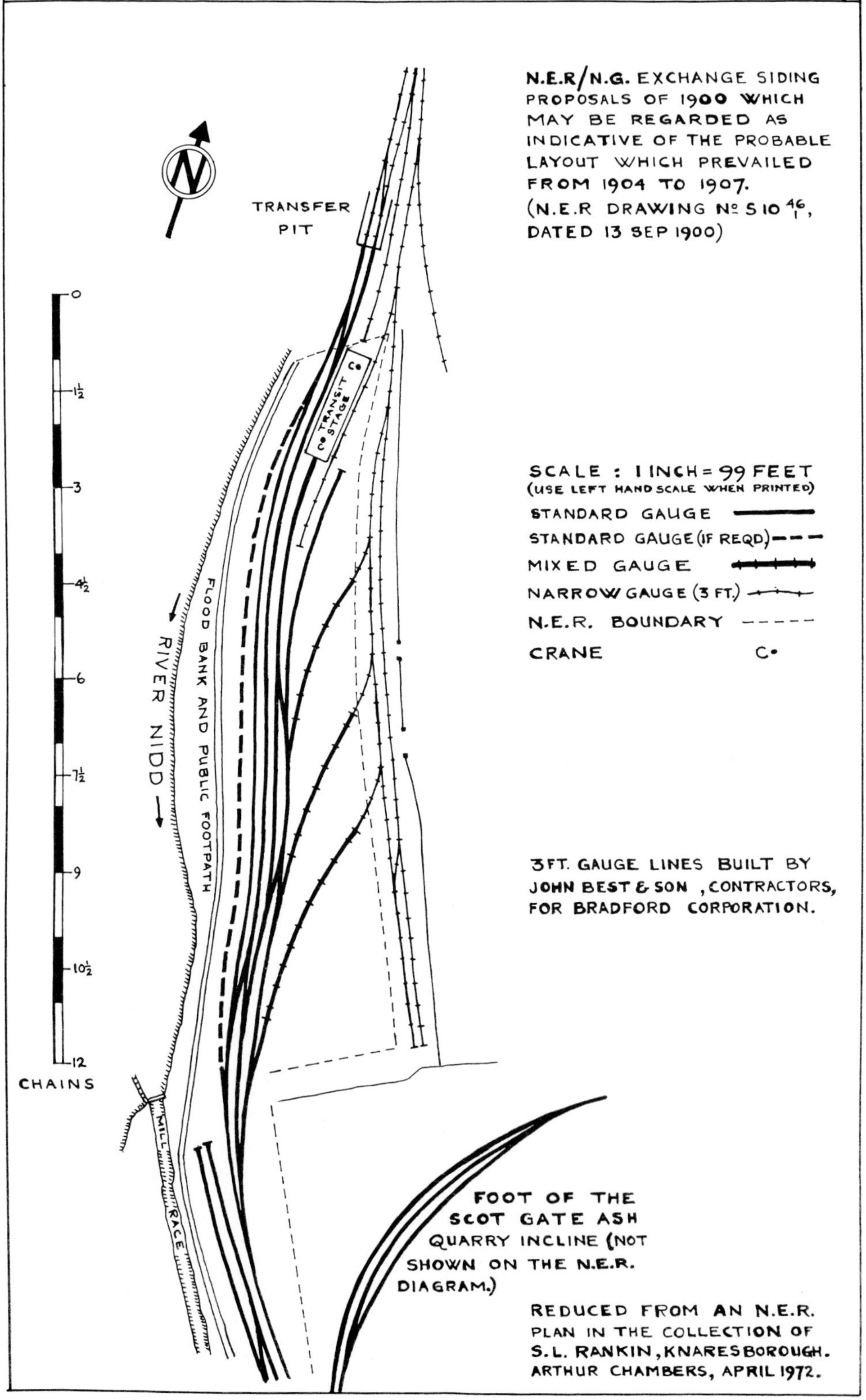

TRANSFER PIT

N.E.R/N.G. EXCHANGE SIDING PROPOSALS OF 1900 WHICH MAY BE REGARDED AS INDICATIVE OF THE PROBABLE LAYOUT WHICH PREVAILED FROM 1904 TO 1907. (N.E.R DRAWING No S10 $^{46}/_1$, DATED 13 SEP 1900)

TRANSIT STAGE

SCALE : 1 INCH = 99 FEET
(USE LEFT HAND SCALE WHEN PRINTED)
STANDARD GAUGE ———
STANDARD GAUGE (IF REQD) ----
MIXED GAUGE ++++++
NARROW GAUGE (3 FT.) +++++
N.E.R. BOUNDARY -----
CRANE   C●

FLOOD BANK AND PUBLIC FOOTPATH

RIVER NIDD →

3 FT. GAUGE LINES BUILT BY JOHN BEST & SON, CONTRACTORS, FOR BRADFORD CORPORATION.

0
1½
3
4½
6
7½
9
10½
12
CHAINS

MILL RACE

FOOT OF THE SCOT GATE ASH QUARRY INCLINE (NOT SHOWN ON THE N.E.R. DIAGRAM.)

REDUCED FROM AN N.E.R. PLAN IN THE COLLECTION OF S.L. RANKIN, KNARESBOROUGH.
ARTHUR CHAMBERS, APRIL 1972.

stone was locomotive worked from its foot onwards to Angram and there dispersed by rail, or 'blondin' and derricks as required.

Small dams and weirs were built (by a subcontractor, Harry Dawson of Kirkby Malzeard) across Stone Beck and the Nidd, with provision for diverting the streams into by-wash channels skirting the future lake. The Nidd was thus connected to the north channel and Stone Beck to the south channel – see map. An old-fashioned steam excavator dug the channels and the residuum lodges (settling tanks) adjoining the dams. Stone had to be brought by rail for lining these channels and other works. Best extended his 3ft gauge north and south of the reservoir to carry stone to the by-washes, lodges and dams. By this time the 'main line' was running on standard gauge and 3ft locos BUNTY, ANGRAM and the old Black Hawthorn FIREFLY worked alongside the by-washes and thus penetrated farther into the wilderness than the other locomotives.

James Watson, the engineer of the Corporation's water department was located in Bradford and came to site from time to time. H Duncan of the Corporation was based at Pateley Bridge and E S Barlow had the appointment of resident engineer, Angram; he actually lived in the large water department house by the road at Gouthwaite and drove in a horse gig to his office in Lofthouse station yard, going on up to Angram on a locomotive when necessary.

Scar House, which gave its name to a later reservoir, was a stone house on the left hillside about 1½ miles before reaching Angram, and here Allan Best and his wife made their home for the duration of the job; he was the son who had charge of the project. John Best, senior, lived at Warriston House Edinburgh, and stayed with Allan on his visits to Nidderdale. When, in 1906, he converted his firm into a private limited company, it became John Best & Sons Ltd, the shareholders being John Best, Allan Best, John Best junior (occupied superintending other projects) and Finlay Best (who went abroad and did not play an active part in the firm). Allan Best had a motor-car, believed of French make, and would drive down to the Lofthouse office. By this time standard gauge was in and Johnny Kelly would bring an engine down to Lofthouse to convey Allan, or sometimes his father, up to Angram site: the Bests insisted on engine-driving themselves on these trips, and drove like mad up the winding line. If it was a Monday morning there might be two or three flat 'bogies' rattling along behind. These were brought up from Lofthouse on Monday or on Friday night for the convenience of the young folk of Angram village who would ride down on them by gravity on Saturday afternoon, have tea in Lofthouse or often walk over the moorland road to Masham and back before trekking home to Angram. Mr W J Sloan, of Bolton, recalled that when newly married in 1915, he and his wife visited his uncle and aunt who lived in one of Best's houses and they rode back on a 'bogie'!

On Saturdays, one of Best's engines worked a passenger train for shoppers from Angram to Lofthouse. Usually passengers changed there into the Corporation's train on the N.V.L.R. but, if circumstances demanded it, Best's train would be taken over at Lofthouse by a Corporation locomotive and worked through to Pateley Bridge – whither his locomotives only worked on goods trains. The passenger train returned to Angram in the evening. This raises the question of what passenger stock was used in those days. There is a suggestion that Best also ran a passenger train on Thursdays.

Mr Woodrup, of Bewerley, lived in those days at a farm near the line, below Scar House, and went to Angram village school; he has told that the enginemen were very friendly and often stopped to give the children a lift to or from school.

The high winds from Whernside have been mentioned. Winter frosts held up concrete work, often for months, and in February 1907 it was reported that many men were out of work at Angram due to a long and continuous storm; the contractor was giving bread and soup once a day and the Corporation drew on the canteen fund to provide bare sustenance. Reports from later winters were in the same vein. Mrs Maria Best, wife of Allan, collected for a 'Navvy Emergency Fund' and in September 1907 wrote from Scar House to thank the Corporation water committee for a gift to the fund.

Best's standard gauge locomotives, to be described, worked between the N.V.L.R. sidings at Pateley Bridge and Angram site, also as mentioned with stone from the quarry incline foot near Scar House to Angram, and on the standard gauge tracks at Angram (the by-wash lines higher up were never converted to standard gauge). The heaviest traffic was cement, and this came in bulk from time to time and was usually conveyed with two locomotives in front and two in rear. Much work was put in at site to unload overnight if necessary in order to return the wagons within three days and avoid demurrage. Best was not authorised to run over the N.E.R. link line at Pateley to the N.E.R. station yard. However, in April 1908 he received a severe reprimand in writing from the water committee: it had come to their notice that a few days before a contractor's engine had run to and from the N.E.R. and they made it clear that if this irregularity should occur again, the contractor would be charged as if for traffic taken over by a N.V.L.R. engine! Murdy McKay was Best's senior driver; he went back later to Scotland. Best had a wooden locomotive shed at Pateley, burned down one evening in a spectacular fire; fortunately, the locomotives had some steam and escaped. It was replaced by the Corporation's iron shed.

In July 1908 John Best, senior, died, but Allan continued in charge and saw to it that the contract was carried through.

The years slipped by. The Council made their last annual pre-war visit to view the progress of the works on 21 July 1914. On 2 June 1915 the water committee went up and reported the works nearly complete and they discussed the proposed new reservoir at Scar House. The committee's visit of 31 May 1916 was to see the Angram reservoir complete (it had overflowed in the preceding January), and the waterworks engineer stated that the contract had been satisfactorily carried out. The population at Angram village had run down, the schoolmaster had 'joined the colours' and the school was closed by June 1916 and in December that year the services of the West Riding police constable were dispensed with. John Best & Sons Ltd received their certificate of completion on 4 August 1917. The contract of 18 December 1903 between the Corporation and John Best specified a price of £365,492.16.6d. The work had been completed at a cost of £372,760. 2.6d. and this included the extra cost of granite imported for large decorative stones at the dam,

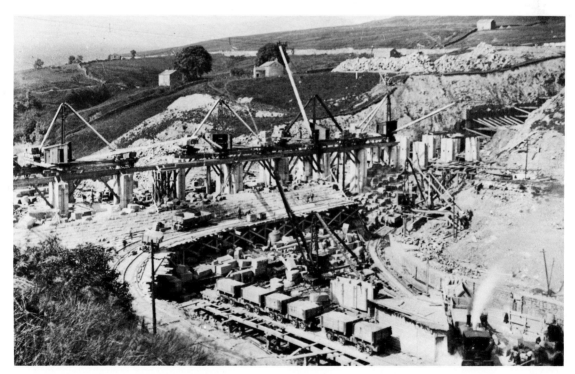

Looking up-valley, the line of Angram dam is marked by the crane gantry across the valley and the timbered trench cut deep into the northern hillside. This busy scene, in September 1910, follows six years work in all weathers. A Barclay 'pug' loco blows off (right).

presumably where the plaque is installed; no wonder that James Watson expressed pleasure at costs held steady for nearly fourteen years.

In April 1919 Mr W J Sloan came home from the Services and lived until September 1919 with his aunt Mrs Bessie Sloan in his uncle's house above Scar but most of Best's houses had been dismantled. Mr W J Sloan was helping with Best's arrangements for sale of plant. During this period the 'blondin' was dismantled and electric cables taken down, power having been cut off at an earlier date. The main line of Best's railway remained in 1919. In September 1920 John Best & Sons held a sale (not their first) and they advertised two saddle tank locomotives, one standard gauge and one 3ft gauge, lying at Pateley Bridge, N.V.L.R.

The identification of these two 'surviving' locomotives can be considered when studying the reconstructed list of John Best's locomotives used at Angram – see later – but may defy conclusive establishment.

Angram dam is now seen from the north, the valve tower prominent, in maybe 1911, with progress since 1910. Note the massive masonry being set in concrete. A saddle tank loco on four passenger carriages provides a train for the visiting party.

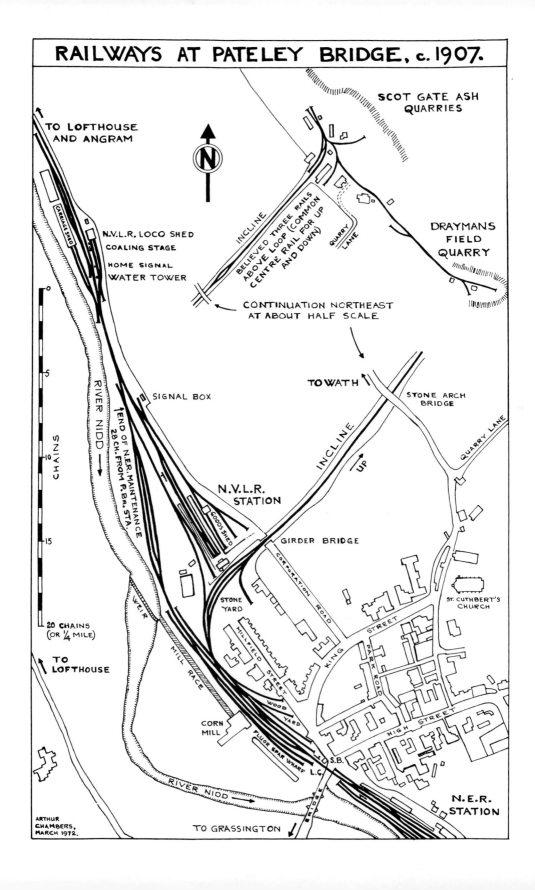

Chapter Fifteen

The Nidd Valley Light Railway: Construction, Equipment, Inauguration and Early Days

Progress with the building (by John Best) of the Bradford Corporation's standard gauge Light Railway between Pateley Bridge N.V.L.R. yard and Lofthouse has been reported in describing the day when the ceremonial first sod was turned, 13 July 1904. During the next month or two the Corporation's sub-committee indulged in trips which would appeal to present-day railway enthusiasts; their object was to gain hints on the working of contemporary Light Railways. They reported on visits to the Vale of Rheidol Railway (gauge 1ft 11½in, opened 1902), the Welshpool and Llanfair Light Railway (gauge 2ft 6in, opened 1903), the Tanat Valley Light Railway (a contemporary standard gauge branch, leased by Cambrian Railways) and the Kent and East Sussex Railway (standard gauge, opened 1900–1904). The last-mentioned was one of the railways managed by Colonel H F Stephens. The waterworks engineer and the Assistant Town Clerk made the pilgrimage to Tonbridge to see 'Mr H Stephens,' described as the 'Engineer and Managing Director'. He was, however, absent and his assistant was helpful. Would this, in 1904, be the redoubtable Mr W H Austen, whose courteous reception I recall – many years later, long after the Colonel's death, in the cramped office with its faded photographs of the outposts of the Stephens empire?

Passenger stations were built at Pateley Bridge, Wath, Ramsgill and Lofthouse on the 6½ miles long line and each had substantial two-storey stone buildings, still to be seen. A carriage shed was ordered for Pateley Bridge, also four goods sheds for the line. John Best was to build the signal box at Pateley Bridge, the only one. Saunders & Co Ltd secured the contract for signalling at Pateley Bridge (£434.15.0d.), the signals having corrugated steel arms. Tyer's electric train tablet equipment, with six instruments, was ordered (£360) and installed. Ground frames on the platforms were employed at Wath, Ramsgill and Lofthouse and these stations also had basic signalling. Wath and Ramsgill were crossing places.

Six open wagons (£373.10.0d.) and two brake vans (£282), all these vehicles surprisingly stated to have Westinghouse brakes but surely really vacuum, were ordered from Hurst, Nelson & Co Ltd of Motherwell, in December 1905, to be painted grey and lettered 'B.C.' in white. On 14 November 1905 the sub-committee had visited the Metropolitan Railway at Neasden to inspect rolling stock displaced by electrification, which had been largely completed by September 1905. They selected ten coaches, four-wheeled, 28ft 4in long, 8ft 6in wide, 12ft high and weighing 10½ tons, with upper frames in oak, body frames and panels in teak, fitted with gas lighting and automatic vacuum brakes. The coaches were described as 'modern' and comprised –

two first class with four compartments
two second class
one first/second composite
three third class with five compartments
two third class with four compartments and van

The price agreed was £800, plus cost of repainting at Neasden. Metropolitan Railway coach numbers 302–10 and 344 have been quoted. The coaches came painted red (Met. lake).

Also selected at the same time were two locomotives, to be thoroughly overhauled and have cabs fitted and condensing gear removed, £1,350 inclusive price for the two (plus spares extra): these could not be described as modern, even in 1905. They came in 1906 or 1907 as –

No. 1 HOLDSWORTH 4-4-0 Side tank oc 17in x 24in; coupled wheels 5ft 10in
        built by Beyer Peacock No. 707 of 1866
        had been Met. Rly. No. 20 until withdrawn 1905

came newly painted in Met. red but with modified lining, the style shown in photographs reproduced. The number plate was specially cast, and dated 1906!

This loco was put to work on N.V.L.R. passenger trains between Pateley Bridge and Lofthouse from 1907. In April 1920, the late Ken Nunn photographed the loco, out of use, in Pateley shed. In July 1920, it was advertised for sale but in 1921 was supplying steam for a water pump at Scar House dam – and remained with the Corporation for at least 14 more years.

No. 2 MILNER   4–4–0 Side tank oc 17in x 24in; coupled wheels 5ft 10in
built by Beyer Peacock No. 1878 of 1879
had been Met. Rly No. 34 until withdrawn 1905. Particulars essentially as for No. 1, except that No. 1 came with a plain dome and twin column safety valves on the firebox, whereas No. 2 arrived with a bell-mouthed dome with a spring-balance safety valve attached, also a brass safety valve casing to be seen on the firebox. Name was erased in 1909.

It was sold in 1914 to the North Wales Granite Company at their sidings which connected to the L.N.W.R. Holyhead main line on the outskirts of Conway, and was transferred from there to the parent company, Brookes Ltd, Lightcliffe, near Halifax in (probably) 1925 and eventually broken up there circa 1932. In N.W. Granite Co days it acquired nameplates CONWAY and their pattern implied overhaul by Manning Wardle of Leeds on acquisition.

Aldermen Holdsworth and Milner had been prominent in direction of Bradford waterworks since at least 1898.

It was realised when ordering these locomotives that the maximum axle loading of 6½ tons specified in the Light Railway Order would have to be increased. The engines would be of the 'B' class, the weight of which was 38.35 tons empty and 46.6 tons in working order, with 36.7 tons in working order on the coupled wheels. The committee 'glossed' the weight at 'over 42 tons'. When advertising No. 2 MILNER for sale in December 1912, the Railway added the comment 'slightly too heavy'.

The two Metropolitan locomotives and ten coaches arrived at Pateley Bridge N.E.R. together, with one locomotive in steam. Mr McCallum Senior of John Best & Sons drove the whole assembly over the N.E.R. link to the N.V.L.R. exchange sidings.

The Corporation also acquired twelve spartan 4-wheel coaches from the Maryport & Carlisle Railway, but this was after the first world war when construction at Scar House was in prospect; they were intended for workmen's traffic rather than the N.V.L.R as such.

Rather surprisingly, the N.V.L.R. was not officially connected to the N.E.R. until about the end of June 1907 but there must surely have been a working link somewhat before this. On Wednesday 24 July 1907 Colonel von Donop arrived at Pateley Bridge at 9.40 a.m. and made his inspection of the N.V.L.R., namely the line up to Lofthouse, inclusive. Prompt approval to running of passenger traffic was given by the Board of Trade, subject to relatively minor recommendations being met.

Mr W T Croft became secretary to the N.V.L.R., additional to his other duties for the Corporation. Advertisements appeared for staff and, after interviews, appointments were made from 2 September 1907 –

Ted Fawcett of Pateley Bridge   – Station master, Pateley Bridge at 30/– per week, plus house etc.
J H Julian of Bradford   – Station master, Lofthouse at 25/– per week, plus house

The Nidd Valley Light Railway in its earlier days, 1907–circa 1917

Opening day, N.V.L.R., 11 September 1907. The decorated train, with locomotive HOLDSWORTH, ex-Metropolitan Railway 4-4-0 tank, and the Corporation saloon leading, is halted at a west-of-line platform believed to be immediately south of Wath Station (one sees the starting (?) signal for southbound trains).

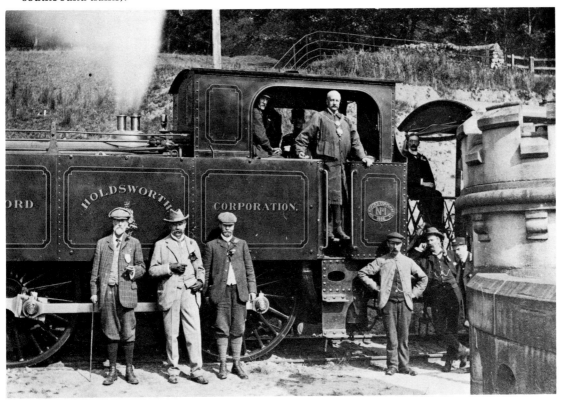

There was a stop at Gouthwaite dam, and refreshments at 'the Aldermen's Rest', calling for a walk to and fro over the dam. Alderman J.A. Goodwin, The Lord Mayor, drove the loco HOLDSWORTH. Standing (L to R) are: James Watson, the engineer; Allan Best, the son in charge of the Angram project; his father John Best, principal of the firm, who died in July 1908.

At Angram platform, Alderman Goodwin and James Watson are again prominent and the inaugural train of saloon and three Met carriages is seen, during the visit of 11 September 1907. John Best's locomotive now seems to be at the outgoing end of the train.

Let us look next at Lofthouse, a 'through' station but terminal for the purpose of the N.V.L.R. The buildings are here seen from the railway side (Angram to left, Pateley to right), with a smartly dressed and anticipatory throng. The signal lever frame is hidden by the crowd.

Leonard Farrer of Bradford	– Porter – S.M., Wath at 25/– plus house etc.
Charles E Wade of Ripley	– Porter – S.M., Ramsgill at 25/– plus house etc.
Fred Robinson of Rawdon	– Porter, Pateley Bridge at 20/– and uniform
H Whitehead of Bradford	– Guard, at 25/– and uniform
Arthur Storey of Bradford	– Engine driver, at 40/–
George Hockley of Bradford	– Stoker (sic), at 30/–
C H Lee of Bradford	– Cleaner, at 23/–
David Garnett of Pateley Bridge	– Platelayer, at 23/–
Abraham Lockwood of Pateley Bridge	– Platelayer, at 23/–

Mr Storey, the engine driver, afterwards withdrew his application and in his stead the Corporation appointed George Albert Pearson, who came from the Midland Railway's Manningham shed in Bradford. Clothing bought from Brown, Muff & Co. Ltd, the well-known Bradford store, embraced lounge suits and caps for station masters, 'corduroy lounge suits', sleeved waistcoats and caps for porters, a lounge suit, sleeved waistcoat and cap for the guard, overcoats for enginemen, cleaners and platelayers.

The ceremonial opening of the N.V.L.R. took place on 11 September 1907 and the main feature of the day was a journey over the line and on to Angram. Starting from Pateley Bridge N.V.L.R. station the Metropolitan tank engine No. 1 HOLDSWORTH was driven by the Lord Mayor of Bradford, Alderman J A Goodwin. The train comprised the Corporation's saloon and three coaches, decorated. Calls were made at Wath; and also to view Gouthwaite compensation reservoir and to take light refreshments at 'The Alderman's Rest' – doubtless the Waterworks house. The next stop was at Lofthouse station where one of John Best's locomotives probably No. 15 GAMESHOPE took over from HOLDSWORTH and worked the train on to Angram. Luncheon was served in the reading room at Angram village. In addition to the Lord Mayor, the civic party included Alderman Holdsworth, chairman of the water committee, whose name the Corporation's engine carried. The Corporation's engineers James Watson, E S Barlow and H Duncan were present and Allan Best represented the contractors who, it will be recalled, built the N.V.L.R. and were in process of building the reservoir at Angram. W T Croft, secretary of the railway, was there. From the contemporary railway scene came: W G Hawkins, Midland Railway district superintendent, Leeds; W Noble, superintendent of Leeds District, N.E.R.; R L Tudor, Midland Railway stationmaster, Bradford; Mr Ascough, district inspector, N.E.R.; Mr Grant, N.E.R. station master, Pateley Bridge. R A Smith, secretary of the Power & Traction Company, was invited; it is not known whether he attended.

Public passenger traffic on the N.V.L.R. commenced next day, fares being –

Journey	Single		Return		Return Excursion	
	1st	3rd	1st	3rd	1st	3rd
Pateley Bridge–Wath	3d	1½d	6d	3d	6d	3d
Pateley Bridge–Ramsgill	8d	4d	1/4d	8d	1/–	6d
Pateley Bridge–Lofthouse	1/–	6d	2/–	1/–	1/6	9d

Season ticket rates were fixed in October 1907.

Goods and mineral charges on the N.V.L.R. were to be as in the N.E.R.'s 1892 scale, plus 25 per cent, which surcharge had been authorised by the Light Railway Order of 1901.

The route is shown on the accompanying map and mileages from Pateley Bridge N.V.L.R. station were approximately 1½ to Wath, 4½ to Ramsgill and 6½ to Lofthouse. Best's line continued for another 6½ miles or thereabouts. The level crossings were protected by cattle guards, not gates. Signalling arrangements have been mentioned. At Pateley, the N.V.L.R. had a locomotive shed of two roads, built in corrugated iron, with coal stage and water tower, in addition to the carriage shed. There was a second locomotive shed at Lofthouse. Before September 1907 was out it was decided to obtain oil lamps for the passenger carriages, so use of the gas lamps was presumably not considered practicable. Further decisions were (12 December 1907) to alter

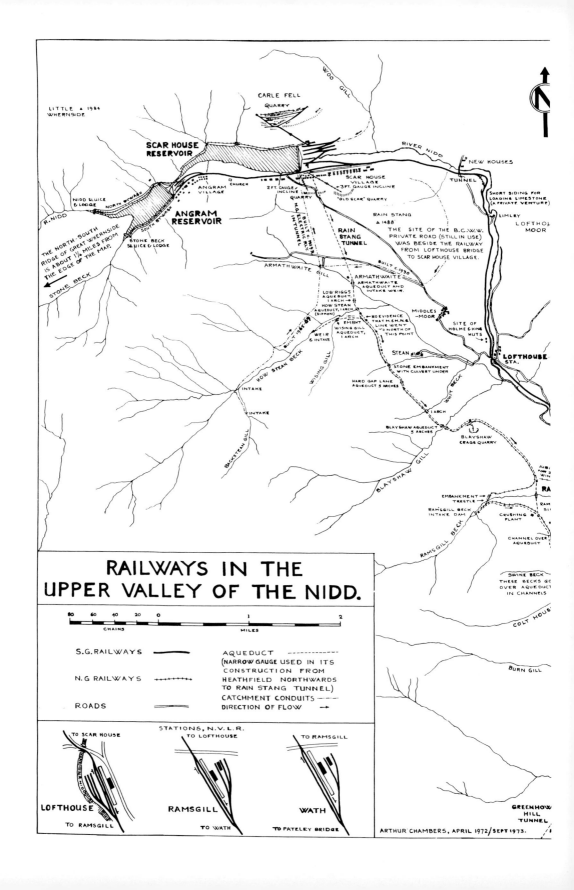

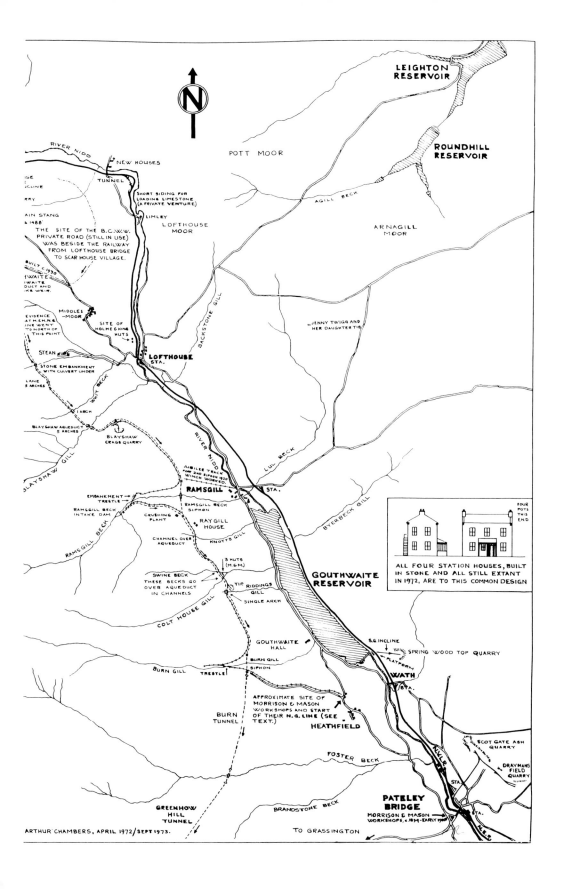

'Lofthouse' to 'Lofthouse-in-Nidderdale' owing to confusion of parcels traffic with other Lofthouses! From February 1908, on representations from the N.E.R's goods manager, 'Wath' was changed to 'Wath-in-Nidderdale.'

A belated sequel to the opening was a letter from Bradford and District United Temperance Council to the City Council protesting at the expenditure on intoxicating drinks in connection with the opening of the N.V.L.R. Looking back, it seems that bills were approved as follows –

Hammonds Brewery Company	– beer and spirits	£94.10.9d.
J Metcalfe & Son Ltd	– beer	£60.9.8d.
J Best & Sons Ltd	– provisions and meat	£2.4.9d.

Presumably the last figure is misleading and does not indicate a lack of sustenance for the distinguished company.

Although the staff originally appointed were mostly very faithful to the N.V.L.R. down the years, there were the inevitable incidents. At Easter 1909, Guard Whitehead refused to clean the carriages and left without notice. On 26 October 1909 the stationmaster at Lofthouse was dismissed on account of irregularities in the books.

Another angle on Lofthouse station is seen. The road in foreground has been newly made by the Corporation but is to be handed over to the local authority early in 1908 – and familiar in the 1990s as the public dale road, with museum and like activity in the building nowadays. The throng is even better seen, clearly out for a special summer occasion. As originally published, this and the previous view claim to depict the opening of Lofthouse station. The train comprises the saloon and *four* Met coaches. A third view, not reproduced, shows a Best Barclay 0-4-0 saddle tank engine on the near (up-valley) head of the train, the locomotive be-flagged. These views do not seem to accord with the ceremonial occasion of 11 September 1907. Maybe they feature one of the first nominally public trains, which began to run on 12 September 1907, but clearly the train shown is to run forward to Angram.

Turning back down-dale from Lofthouse, a service train on the N.V.L.R. is here calling at Ramsgill station, ex-Met 4-4-0 tank locomotive running bunker first. The goods shed is in situ and open for use and the picture was on card permitting a halfpenny stamp – so the scene is in the early years. The church is in Bouthwaite village.

This view is eastward across the valley to Wath-in-Nidderdale station, Pateley Bridge being rightwards. Again, the goods shed indicates early days of the N.V.L.R. In the background are probably Howson Ridge (L) and High Ruckles (1212ft, R).

An interesting but slightly obscure chapter in the early history of the N.V.L.R. concerned excursion traffic from the N.E.R. In November 1906 James Watson had discussed with N.E.R. officials and also with Lt. Colonel P G von Donop at the Board of Trade in London the prospect of excursion passenger traffic passing over the goods yard and sidings between Pateley Bridge N.E.R. station and the N.V.L.R. but the outcome was inconclusive. Later in the same month the Corporation and the N.E.R. submitted a joint letter to the Board of Trade asking permission for such traffic to pass twice every week during the months of June, July, August and September. By a letter of 14 December 1906 the B.O.T. agreed to not more than three excursions per week during June, July, August and September 1907 running through to get onto the N.V.L.R. An agreement on this topic between the Corporation and the N.E.R. was drafted and redrafted and final 'Heads of Agreement' approved on 3 May 1907 – all in good time before the official opening to normal passenger traffic. On 3 September 1907 the N.E.R. wrote to say that they would provide dual brake fitted stock for excursion traffic, evidently visualising their own engines using the Westinghouse brake and the Corporation's engines vacuum brake. On Saturday 14 September 1907, a few days after the opening, the first N.E.R. excursion was booked to run to Pateley Bridge and Lofthouse but someone must have had cold feet in the typical railway tradition and in the event the N.E.R. would not run their stock through to Lofthouse nor allow the Corporation engine and carriages to come to the N.E.R. platform – the N.E.R. thus failed to comply with the Heads of Agreement. The excursionists would have to make their way between the stations at their own expense, or inconvenience. However, it was agreed in time for the summer of 1908 that the N.E.R. would issue through excursion tickets to Wath-in-Nidderdale, Ramsgill and Lofthouse-in-Nidderdale, retaining a commission of 5 per cent for costs of advertising and ticket issuing. A specific excursion, early in the 1908 season, was for a party from Allerton – a colliery district of Yorkshire; this party evidently planned a rail trip right through to Angram – presumably to view the works and maybe enjoy a picnic – and the Corporation sub-committee agreed to lend John Best two N.V.L.R. carriages and a brake van, subject to indemnities by Best; the Council was later unhappy about this arrangement.

On another quiet day, a passenger train from Lofthouse has arrived at Pateley Bridge station, with Met carriages, the terminal building prominent, the goods yard and shed glimpsed to left.

At the close of 1908 it was reported that the Metropolitan locomotive MILNER was not running smoothly and tenders were invited for supply of a new locomotive. On 3 March 1909 the Water sub-committee viewed a locomotive at Leeds Steel Works made by Andrew Barclay and, at the works of Hudswell Clarke in Leeds, a new engine for the Mid Suffolk Light Railway was inspected. The furnaces of Walter Scott Ltd, Leeds Steel Works, were in the Hunslet district. Their locomotive was presumably AB 639 of 1889, a four-coupled machine with 13in cylinders and perhaps being offered for sale in anticipation of the coming of a new one from Hawthorn Leslie. The engine seen at Hudswell Clarke's works in Hunslet would be a new one, 0-6-0 Side tank with inside cyls. 13in x 20in HC 867 of 1909, which went to the Mid Suffolk Light Railway as their No. 3 and was called into Stratford when the L.N.E.R. took over on 1 July 1924, but was condemned without receiving an L.N.E.R. number – unlike its two slightly older sisters from Hudswells, which put in service as L.N.E.R. Nos. 8316/7 for a few years. The sub-committee promptly ordered a comparable new locomotive of Hudswell design but with outside cylinders, at a price of £1,330: it was to be delivered with nameplates MILNER and would replace the old MILNER (which, as noted previously, stayed on and then moved to a fresh career). Thus we have delivered on 26 May 1909 –

MILNER   0-6-0 Side tank oc 12in x 18in – 3ft 3in coupled wheels
by Hudswell Clarke 882 of 1909
going into service, with vacuum brake, screw couplings and safety chains, as the principal passenger engine on the N.V.L.R., stationed at Pateley Bridge, and working as such until the line acquired a railcar in 1921. MILNER then moved to Scar village, for use on workmen's passenger trains and goods trains until the

The replacement loco MILNER, by Hudswell Clarke 1909, in its pre-first world war days on passenger duties, N.V.L.R., the vacuum brake hose prominent. Personalities figure: Tom Watson; Albert Pearson, previously of Manningham engine shed, Midland Railway, who served as driver, N.V.L.R., 1907–1937; Mr Hulse, by the buffer beam; Arthur Calvert, porter; William Chadwick; George Hockley, fireman from 1907 until probably 1913; Leonard Farrer, porter/stationmaster, Wath (the last two on the footplate).

completion of the project at Scar. It is reported that the locomotive passed to Sir Lindsay Parkinson & Sons Ltd and was employed by them, as 328 MILNER, on the construction of the Royal Ordnance Factory, Chorley, c. 1937–39. I saw the loco on 8/2/1941, still as MILNER, at Northolt, engaged on the widening and electrification for London Transport trains to Ruislip; the makers note the owners in 12/1943 as Caffin & Company, Ruislip. At some later date, the makers bought the loco back and, after repairs by them, including new firebox, it was sold in 8/1947 to George Wimpey & Co. Ltd for work at Port Talbot (a contract for steelworks expansion?). Wimpeys became operating contractors to the National Coal Board, at Gurnos opencast coal screens beside the Swansea Vale line and there I renewed acquaintance with the loco, working, on 16/9/1952; by this time, new, wider side tanks had been fitted and the name lost. With wheels 3ft 3in diameter, there was quite a difference from its predecessor MILNER with its 5ft 10in four coupled wheels. The vacuum brake equipment was removed by the makers on sale to Wimpeys in 1947.

The public passenger train service on the N.V.L.R. during its passenger carrying career was usually four trains each way (Sundays excepted) in summer and three each way in winter – with an extra train each way on Wednesdays and Saturdays. In the nineteen-twenties there were five trains.

With the completion of Angram reservoir, not only did passage of construction traffic cease but the consequent run-down of population and activity at Angram reduced the demand for passenger trains on the N.V.L.R. itself, namely south of Lofthouse. By March 1916 three members of the staff had joined the services and application was made to exempt the others from military service in order to keep the railway going.

The later history of the N.V.L.R. will be dealt with in describing the activities at Scar House in the nineteen-twenties and 'thirties.

Saloon carriages on the railway

John Best had a passenger carrying vehicle in the early days, which has been described as a saloon and was dignified by the name of 'Kitty'. It ran on a four wheeled bogie, 3ft gauge, and had a rather square but neatly panelled body with four side windows and at one end a covered verandah. The name was painted on the sides.

The Bradford Corporation felt the need of a coach for special occasions but there has down the years been much confusion in print about it; this may arise from failure by writers to realise that two gauges of railway were involved.

By a minute of 22 February 1904 the waterworks committee approved the purchase from Hurst Nelson & Company Limited of Motherwell, of a 'car' for the railway from Lofthouse to Angram at a cost of £250. This would be for the 3ft gauge. In May 1904 the Board of Trade agreed to standard gauge being adopted for the Nidd Valley Light Railway. The Corporation must have enquired promptly whether their coach, then on order, could be adapted but on 2 June 1904 Hurst Nelson said that the car as ordered could not be altered in gauge. The narrow gauge saloon was duly delivered and a shed was built at Lofthouse to house it. It was carried on four wheels and low built. There were three windows in each side of the body with twin top lights over each, end platforms tramway style and a flat roof extending beyond the ends of the body. Between each window was a decorative panel, the lining was in traditional tramway style and the city arms appeared on the sides. A photograph published by Mr J H Price in *Modern Tramway* of May 1964 was taken in Hurst Nelson's yard about 1910 and shows the body without its end platforms and buffing gear, mounted on a four wheeled truck which may not have been its own. It had been returned to Hurst Nelson and there is a suggestion, not corroborated, that this was in part exchange for another vehicle. In 1912 the old saloon body was fitted up on a standard gauge truck and delivered to the Wantage Tramway, a standard gauge line from Wantage Road station, G.W.R., to Wantage Town, as their No. 5. It is illustrated by Mr F M Atkins on P.187 of *The Railway*

A vehicle from Hurst Nelson, Motherwell builders, 1906.

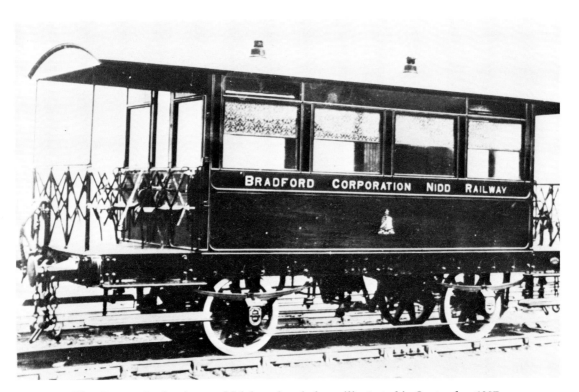

The Corporation's saloon, which has already been illustrated in September 1907.

Magazine for 1928 (second half year) and the decorative panels between the windows are found to be of coloured glass.

A new standard gauge saloon was acquired, almost certainly from Hurst Nelson and very probably in part exchange for the previous coach. There exists a maker's photograph of it and it is on view in the picture of the inaugural standard gauge train at Angram in 1907, so it had been delivered by 11 September 1907. It had four wheels, four side windows in the body, open end platforms, with small seats on them and concertina gates, two oil lamps in the roof, vacuum brake and through piping for running in Westinghouse braked trains (of the N.E.R., presumably). It was lettered on the waist 'Bradford Corporation Nidd Valley' and carried the arms on the lower sides of the body. It is understood to have been used for very special occasions and the water committee's annual visits, but not usually in between nor for the engineer's journeys.

Steam railmotors

In view of the much later coming of a second-hand steam railcar, it is interesting that in 1909 the Corporation put out enquiries for a steam railmotor to two firms, neither of which is familiar to the writer as a builder of such vehicles. Mountain and Gibson of Bury quoted for a car 30ft long and 8ft wide, to hold 56 people, £1,300. John Milliken of Belfast offered a car 27ft long and 8ft 3in wide, for 40 passengers, at £1,175. No purchase was made at the time.

Not many of these selected N.V.L.R. tickets show a date on the face, but 1910 appears.

Chapter Sixteen

The Scar House Era, 1913–1936

Scar House: preliminary arrangements 1913–1920

As Angram dam approached completion, the Corporation of Bradford reviewed their waterworks projects of 1891–92 and by Section 13 of their 1913 Act secured authority to abandon the plan for a reservoir to be called High Woodale and to build a new and much larger reservoir near Scar House (home for some years of Allan Best and his wife). It was to incorporate and submerge the Haden Carr reservoir, which had been built in the last decade of the nineteenth century. The powers were brief and wide, with no specific reference to railways. They enabled work to start when appropriate. An Act of 1925 elaborated, referring to the authorities given by Act of 1890 as amended by the Acts of 1892 and 1913 (above) and authorised a revised Scar House dam, 'also tramroads, railways, sidings ... in connection with ... the waterworks.'

In December 1919 the City Council approved an estimate of £2,161,500 for the works. Nevertheless, tenders were invited and three received, but on 14 May 1920, after lengthy consideration, it was resolved to construct the works by direct labour, under the control of the waterworks engineer. James Watson, waterworks engineer throughout the Angram project, had died on 29 March 1919 and his successor was Lewis Mitchell, whose salary was increased by an extra £1,000 per annum from 1 July 1920 for an estimated fifteen years as administrator of Scar House reservoir construction, in conjunction with the chairman and deputy chairman of the water committee. John Busfield was the first resident engineer on Scar House works, succeeded circa 1924 by William Newlands.

Scar village: 1920–1921

In July 1920 plans were agreed for a new village, to be built on the rising slopes to the south of the 'main line', just short of Scar House and the site of the dam which was to take its name. The 'temporary' but well designed and substantial buildings had a good deal in common with that other excellent hillside village, Ewden, near Sheffield (built 1913–14). Walker, of Sheffield, is understood to have had a hand in both Ewden and Scar villages; the building of Scar village was shared between Newton Chambers (the larger timber buildings), Cowiesons (various timber bungalows) and Vickers (the steel-framed buildings). The plan of Scar House construction site gives an idea of the scale and layout of the village – first one came to East View with its blocks of residential units, the schoolmaster Mr Holmes and the W.R.C.C. policeman Mr Tate being at one time amongst residents here; then followed the ten hostels, each for 64 single men, with a clever layout to suit the different levels and including self-contained living quarters for the landlady and family, servants' rooms, kitchen, men's large dining room, bathrooms, lavatories, lockable sleeping cubicles, a drying room for wet clothes and other refinements. There followed the 'public buildings' – school (opened 9 April 1923), canteen, recreation room, 'concert hall' and the mission church. Then, beyond the course of Best's old quarry incline, of which the last use was to bring some stone down for the village construction, were the 'C' type bungalows, each with bay window and gable, intended for married couples and, below them, the desirable residences in The Crescent: these were a group of 'A' type double-fronted bungalows, each with verandah (gabled) between its opulent bay windows – all fronting on to a semi-circular service road or walkway, separated from the main road by a garden or greensward. Mr George Renton, assistant engineer at the site from its beginning and through the peak period of its activity until 1930, recalled living at No. 3 and later No. 7, The Crescent. Further on again was Scar House, then occupied by the Corporation's resident engineer, and West View was the last group of residential buildings before the hospitals – which latter dated at least in part from Angram days – apart from one house of the 'Best' period which remained just west of the old Middlesmoor road. Charges ranged from 8d per night for accommodation and service in the hostels to rents (inclusive of rates,

A view down the valley from Angram dam (after its completion) and up the ascent from the foot of the dam to join Bests' 'main route' on the upper level. Interesting is the pipeline to the hydro-electric generating station put in at the Haydon Carr site to provide power and lighting current for the Scar House project and its village. It was later supplemented by another power station.

A steam navvy is digging on the site of Scar village. Locomotive PIONEER (soon renamed HAIG), Manning Wardle 1224 of 1891, is on tipping wagons.

At Scar village – an up-valley view on the line of the 10 major hostels, each for 64 men, showing the clever adaptation to the sloping hillside. Each unit comprises sleeping quarters with cubicles (L), lavatory and bathing facilities (centre), dining and kitchen accommodation (R), and quarters for landlady and family (R again, facing road and railway).

Also facing onto 'main street' of Scar Village are (L to R): reading room; cinema; church (this last having been brought down from Angram site village).

DIAGRAM OF SCAR HOUSE RESERVOIR PROJECT, 1920-35.

(A hand-drawn schematic map, not to scale but X to Y ≈ approx. 1 mile.)

Upper section (quarry and incline area):
- CARLE FELL QUARRY
- 2 FT. GAUGE ABOVE FACE (SIMPLEX PETROL LOCO)
- WINDING ENGINE
- SINGLE TRACK INCLINE
- TWO ROAD LOCO SHED
- FIRST QUARRY FACE
- LATER WORKING FACE
- DOUBLE TRACK SELF ACTING INCLINE
- LOCO WORKED INCLINE (c. 1930)
- TWO ROAD LOCO SHED
- EXPLOSIVES STORE
- OLD ROAD TO COVERDALE
- SCAR HOUSE RESERVOIR (ABSORBED HADEN CARR R'VOIR)
- LINE TO ANGRAM CUT BY DAM IN FINAL STAGES (1933) OF SCAR HOUSE CONSTRUCTION.
- MASONRY DAM (ROADWAY ON TOP)
- BLONDIN TOWER
- NEW SCAR HOUSE FOR RESERVOIR KEEPER ON SITE OF INCLINE FOOT
- TRIANGLE LAYOUT FOR TURNING LOCOS
- BARN
- BARN
- CRUSHER
- HIGH WOODALE FARM
- HIGH WOODALE STEAM POWER GENERATING STATION
- STONEYARD
- LOCO SHED
- CONCRETE MIXER
- CEMENT SHED
- CONCRETE MIXER CEMENT SHED
- BLONDIN CONNECTED THE TWO MIXERS
- THIS DESCENDING LINE NOW A ROAD
- SHOPS CEMENT SHED, MIXER
- FRIED FISH SHOP
- SCHOOL CANTEEN READING ROOM CINEMA CHURCH
- LAUNDRY BAKEHOUSE
- MARRIED QUARTERS (6 HOUSES AND 11 PAIRS)
- THE CRESCENT
- TEN HOSTELS (SINGLE MEN)
- GOOSEWAGE WORKS SLAUGHTERHOUSE
- CARRIAGE SHED ROOM FOR SPARE LOCO
- EAST VIEW 18 HOUSES IN THREE BLOCKS
- PRESENT ROAD
- RIVER NIDD
- TO LOFTHOUSE →
- THE SITE OF THE B.C.W. PRIVATE ROAD (STILL IN USE) THE RAILWAY WAS BESIDE FROM LOFTHOUSE BRIDGE TO SCAR VILLAGE.
- TO ANGRAM (LATER ROAD)
- MORTUARY. ISOLATION HOSPITAL.
- HOSPITAL.
- HUT FROM JOHN BEST'S WORK OCCUPIED BY MR. ADAM SLOAN. WEST VIEW (FOUR MARRIED QUARTERS).
- SCAR HOUSE, OCCUPIED BY ENGINEER, JOHN BEST, JNR. PRESENT STONE BUNGALOW.
- PUBLIC ROAD
- COAL STAGE
- S.P.
- TO MIDDLESMOOR
- 2 FT. GAUGE INCLINE
- 3 FT. GAUGE INCLINE
- "OLD SCAR" QUARRY, USED FOR ANGRAM.
- QUARRY, USED FOR HADEN CARR.

Key – BUILDINGS NEAR THE DAM:
- A: OCTAGONAL STONE MEASURING HOUSE.
- B: SAWMILL.
- C: CARPENTERS' SHOP / WAGONS
- D: SITE OFFICE.
- E: STORES
- F: FITTING SHOP.
- P: PLATFORM.

THE RAILWAY RAN UP THE PRESENT ROAD WHEN BUILDING SCAR VILLAGE.

NOT TO SCALE, BUT X TO Y = APPROX. 1 MILE.

N ↑

ARTHUR CHAMBERS, MARCH 1973.

water and electric light) of 7/– per week for type 'C' (three rooms), 8/– per week for type 'B' and 9/– per week for type 'A' bungalows – all the bungalows having also bathroom and W.C., scullery, pantry, storeroom, coal house and hot and cold water apparatus. In general, the buildings were in timber, gabled, with red asbestos roof tiles and blue Staffordshire ridge tiles. On this bleak site even the Crescent bungalows had their faults. The icy east wind penetrated the bay windows and whistled under the five doors (including bathroom and a bedroom) which opened to the kitchen.

The canteen, with separate portions for workmen, foremen and gangers, and visitors, had its own cellars and a house attached for the manager. The recreation room incorporated a billiard room with two tables and a reading and writing room with newspapers; in February 1923 a branch of Bradford Free Libraries was opened and 5,000 volumes issued in a year to 450 members. The 'concert hall' included stage and dressing rooms, cinema projection (the projection box found surviving in situ in 1972) and was used also for whist drives and dances. It was here that Dr. Flintoff and Pateley Bridge Operatic Society put on a Gilbert and Sullivan opera annually.

The mission church was taken down at Angram and re-erected here at Scar village, being purchased by the Corporation in April 1922 for £150, from the Industrial Christian Fellowship – 'the Navvy Mission Society'. In addition to services taken by the resident missioner, Mr Coplestone, who had been missioner on projects in Wales and earlier at King George Dock, Southampton, others were taken by Father Hammond of Harrogate (weekly) and the Vicar of Middlesmoor (monthly communion). There was a harmonium in the church and a small choir was formed. The service alternated between 'Church' and 'Plain', titles which distinguished between Church of England and nonconformist services. The Roman Catholic priest celebrated mass in the canteen building. Later, 1934, the mission church moved yet again to new pastures; that tale of another 40 years is told in sequence.

The bakery (see plan) could produce 200 loaves per hour and the nearby laundry was in corrugated iron and cunningly contrived from the goods shed buildings formerly at Wath and Ramsgill stations.

The shopping centre, lower down the hill, provided a block of six shops – hairdresser/newsagent, greengrocer/fishmonger, drapery store, grocery store, butcher's and boot repairer's, all let to and run by Marrison and Company of Bradford, goods for the stores being conveyed free by the Corporation's railway. The fried fish and chip potato shop was, prudently, a separate building. A sub-post-office and bank were provided too. Electric lighting was at 110 volts D.C. There were tennis courts, but the recognised football field was at Ramsgill; presumably there was no adequate level ground at Scar village and Ramsgill would be more accessible to visiting teams in the Harrogate Football league, to which the home team was affiliated.

The village, mostly completed by the end of 1921, has been described fairly fully by the writer owing to being one of the best of its kind and era, and giving an idea of the stable background against which the construction works and railway operation may be viewed.

Reconditioning the railways, 1920–1921

In March 1920 electrification of the Nidd Valley Light Railway, with hydro-electric generation, was considered but turned down on economic grounds. The surviving Metropolitan tank locomotive HOLDSWORTH was considered unduly heavy and was offered for sale in 1920. There were no buyers and she was sent up to Scar and (as mentioned earlier) put in a spell of stationary duty. Also in March 1920 the Hudswell tank MILNER was to be overhauled, and purchase of a light steam locomotive and two steam railmotor cars was to be considered.

Amongst staff on the N.V.L.R. in 1920 were A McCallum with the title of foreman and Albert Roper as yard foreman. Wath and Ramsgill lost their goods facilities around this time and the ground floors of the station buildings were converted to houses. On the line above Lofthouse, right through to Angram, improvements were commenced around August 1920. Many curves were eased and track reformed and improved. A loop was put in near Lofthouse and another at Woodale, on the approach to the new Scar House layout. A major work was making a tunnel 180

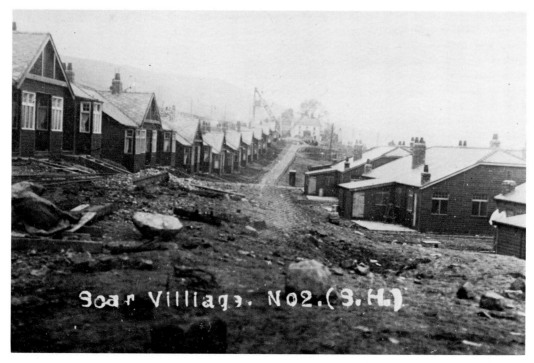

Further westward, up-valley, in Scar Village, the married quarters (L) and backs of the bungalows in the Crescent (R) are seen before landscaping. Distant is the south tower of the 'blondin', its ropeway crossing the dam alignment through the mists to the right.

After landscaping and in occupation, this is the prime residential accommodation in the Crescent, Scar Village.

The shopping centre in Scar Village is nearing completion. The main railway route is below, on the far (lower) side of the shops, but a loop line was in use for a time along the 'main street' (foreground).

'The Walking ganger', as sketched by David T. Rose, engineer with Bradford Corporation in upper Nidderdale, 1920s–1930s.

yards long, the first on the line (apart from the one-time temporary penetration of Angram dam), near the quarry at Goydin Pot (Goyden Pot on o.s. map). Mr George Renton has told of setting out this tunnel, difficult owing to the trees on the hill above. The tunnel eased the curve and was subsequently used for ascending trains, but trains coming down the valley usually took the old, sharply-curved line round the outside of the hill – which had been difficult for heavy trains, especially when carrying long and weighty timbers up the grade. From Lofthouse to Scar House, the railway climbed continuously and gradients were mostly 1 in 40 to 1 in 70. Those on the N.V.L.R., Pateley up to Lofthouse, ranged between 1 in 50 and 1 in 500, also climbing. In general, rails dating from Best's time were 56lbs per yard, flat bottomed, in 33ft lengths and the line ballasted in stone, but it is significant that an inventory of materials in 1932 mentioned 50 tons of 75lbs rails and 30 tons of 50lbs rails, which implies considerable relaying with 75 or 80lbs. Station buildings, signal box, signals, gates and other items were painted red and the whole railway put into a workmanlike state. Be it noted, however, the line above Lofthouse was never part of the Nidd Valley Light Railway.

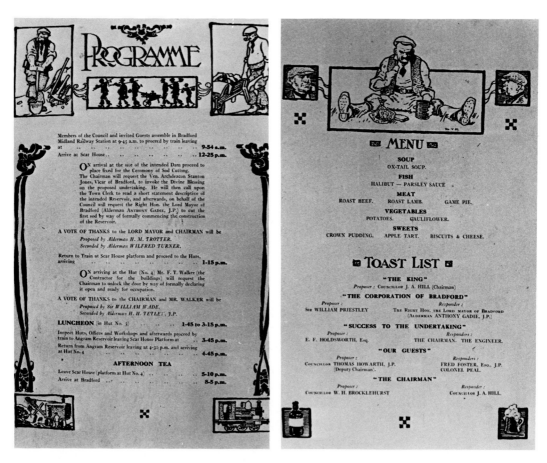

The day's programme and luncheon menu for the sod-cutting occasion at Scar House reservoir, 5 October 1921, repays study. (The timetable of the day is also reproduced in the book's main text). These documents are the work of David Rose, site engineer and artist, and even include a navvy enjoying his 'piece' and liquid refreshment, while silhouettes take in manual and steam digging, and locomotive power.

Minor works at Angram

It was found in 1921 that the southern shore of Angram reservoir was being eroded by wind and waves, in the vicinity of the dam; 'beaching and pitching' were undertaken and the stone was secured by opening up a small quarry close by the bank – shown on plan of Angram. The standard gauge line was extended beyond Angram dam for the first time, following the course of the 3ft gauge between reservoir and catchwater, to reach the new quarry, and this extension lasted for the duration of this minor work, a locomotive running up as required.

The first sod cut at Scar House site, 1921

In order to give the works at Scar House a good start, the City Council of Bradford and their guests carried out a comprehensive programme on 5 October 1921, as follows:–

Bradford Midland Railway station dep 9.54 a.m. by train, joining the Corporation train at Pateley N.V.L.R.
Scar House platform arr 12.25 p.m.
    Cutting of first sod by Ald. Anthony Gadie, J P, Lord Mayor.
Scar House platform (train) dep – short journey to the huts (1.15 p.m.) Councillor J A Hill, Chairman, unlocked the door of Hut No. 4 for occupation.
    Luncheon in Hut No. 3   1.45–3.15 p.m.
    Inspection of huts, offices and workshops.
Scar House platform (train) dep 3.45 p.m. to Angram.
Angram (train) dep 4.30 p.m.
Scar House (Hut No. 4) arr 4.45 p.m.
    Afternoon Tea.
Scar House (platform at Hut No. 4) dep 5.10 p.m.
(a special temporary platform presumably), changing stations at Pateley Bridge.
Bradford arr 8.5 p.m.

Alderman Gadie had served on the committee from the beginning of the Angram project and was to continue to serve, soon as chairman, right on to the end of the Scar scheme. Lewis Mitchell (waterworks engineer) and William Newlands (resident engineer – who in 1930 became the waterworks engineer until completion of the job) were the senior engineers present. Tribute was paid to James Watson (died 1919) who designed the Gouthwaite, Angram and Scar House dams, with (Sir) Alexander Binnie as consultant.

A very attractive menu was produced for this occasion depicting a navvy at his meal, seated on the ground, and pipe-smoking navvies. The programme was decorated with sketches of navvies at work, a steam navvy and a six-coupled outside-cylinder saddle tank locomotive in the 'Peckett' tradition. The artist was D T Rose, who had exhibited at the Royal Academy. He was an engineer with John Best on the building of the Caledonian Railway's Ballachulish branch line at the turn of the century and his career had also embraced port developments in Malta, at Southampton and at Fishguard. At Scar House he was a senior assistant to the resident engineer and responsible for various detailed design work.

Electric power at Scar House dam site

Electric power was required and initially, in 1921, a hydro-electric installation was put in by Vickers Ltd. Water was drawn from Angram reservoir by a steel main 35in to 31in diameter, 4,775ft long, to a power house built on the banks of the Nidd with discharge into Haden Carr reservoir – the site being later submerged by Scar House reservoir. Two water turbines running at 1,000 r.p.m. with a head of 168ft each drove direct a D.C. generator of 250 KVA producing 2,400 volts at 50 cycles, a three phase supply. Overhead lines at 2,400 volts led to substations at the quarry, at each end of the dam site and in the village, to step down the voltage for the respective local needs. The inauguration of this power house brought Alderman Gadie and civic party up for a winter visit on 7 December 1921. The party left the Town Hall at 8.30 a.m. by motor car to reach Pateley Bridge N.V.L.R. station at 9.50 a.m. and there meet Mr Douglas Vickers M.P., chairman, and other representatives of Messrs Vickers Ltd. All travelled by special train right through to Angram, calling briefly 10.30–10.45 a.m. to view the reservoir and intake to the water main, back in the train as far as Vickers' office at Scar House site, then walking down to the power house for the starting-up ceremony by Alderman Gadie and a buffet in the power house. This was by way of light refreshment before climbing back to Vickers' office, taking the train to Scar House platform and motor cars to the Crown Hotel, Middlesmoor for luncheon. The water committee motored all the way back from Middlesmoor to Bradford but the remainder of the party were conveyed by train from Lofthouse (3.0 p.m.) to Pateley Bridge. The reduced use of the M.R., N.E.R. and Corporation trains will be noted.

A steam generating station was built subsequently in order roughly to double the generating capacity at the site. It was at High Woodale, on the north side of the valley downstream of the main site. Two new 'economic' boilers by Davey Paxman & Co Ltd supplied steam to a triple expansion high speed engine by Davey Paxman (driving a 300kw dynamo by Lancashire Dynamo & Motor Co Ltd) and to two Davey Paxman 'Peache' engines (each driving a 100kw dynamo by L.D. & M. Company). The generating plant, except the boilers, came second-hand from Bo'ness Electric Generating Station in Scotland, costing £900. The principal fresh demand for current was from the stone preparation plant near which the power station was located. Inauguration was on 5 June 1925, by which time the quarry was in use and the stone plant being brought into operation. Domestic use of electricity in Scar village was restricted to electric irons and lighting but for cooking and heating coal was used.

The site layout at Scar House

The accompanying plan has been reconstructed to show the complex railway layout developed mostly in 1921–22 to make possible the major dam construction of the ensuing ten

This view is from the Middlesmoor hill road – a peaceable public walkway today but here revealing a scene of activity. Excavation for Scar House dam strikes across the valley northward. Some of the married quarters figure and the stone chimneys of the bungalow show above them. Also seen are offices, workshops, steep zig-zag railways, and the quarry incline on the north side. Our diagram of Scar House projects aids understanding of this and other views.

years. The reason for the zig-zags down to the stream and up the other side was the great difference in levels in a steep-sided valley and photographs reproduced give an idea of the scene at the height of activity – and long afterwards.

It is interesting that during the building of Scar village a line diverged to run along the present private road, higher on the southern hillside than the 'main line', which it rejoined near the dam; a picture in the Corporation's records shows the temporary line passing the new houses in the Crescent.

The associated buildings were erected in 1921–23, the majority on the south side of the valley downstream from the dam site. They included office (including drawing office), stores, fitting shop and smithy 120ft x 30ft, principal locomotive shed 72ft by 30ft with two roads, sawmill and carpenter's shop, wagon shop and cement shed and mixer plant. Most of these premises were in corrugated iron or wood, with steel frames and concrete foundations; the pits and foundations of the locomotive and wagon shops are seen today and so is the loco coal stage. A smaller two-roads locomotive shed, in timber, was sited just north of the stream. A carriage shed with two roads was built at the eastern end of the layout, primarily to accommodate twelve four-wheeled carriages which were bought from the Maryport & Carlisle Railway in, probably, 1922, to provide for workmen's and social travel from Scar Village and site; the first class compartments in this stock were marked 'For Staff'. A main 'blondin' (aerial ropeway) was built to span the valley over the dam site and a lesser one 480 yards down the valley. Each could carry 7 tons in the bucket. They could be dangerous if misused; they were ballasted with pigs of lead, one of which fell out in a high wind and killed a workman who was digging on the dam site.

In close-up. This northward study features the massive concrete of Scar dam, with beyond a glimpse of the incline foot to the quarry. The locomotive is by Hudswell Clarke, doubtless IAN HAMILTON of 1897, which came as TRENT.

On the north side of the valley at Scar, one sees the concrete mixing plant, with stone crushers above, near the foot of the quarry incline. Locomotive MITCHELL (later called ILLINGWORTH) is by Hudswell Clarke, 1916. A Peckett loco tops the scene: KITCHENER, of 1902.

From a higher elevation, locomotives stand below the concrete plant, with the crushers above (R). Westward, up the valley, the massive skeleton of the dam is visible.

Near the incline head, in Carle Fell quarry: the site and pits of the main quarry loco shed appear on 22 May 1971; the characterful Tom Garth was recalling his working days on the vast site.

In working days, the incline head is below (L). At least two working locos, and cranes, are serving the various upper levels of Carle Fell quarry, and the topmost loco shed is silhouetted.

A dramatic descent is being made from Carle Fell to Scar site – and distant Bradford – almost certainly during the civic visit of 5 June 1925.

Scar House dam is nearly finished and limited water is being admitted from mountain streams; note the valve tower, approximately half way along the dam wall, in this southerly view, with the village site across the valley (half left).

The construction of Scar House dam

The foundations for the dam at Scar House were carried down to the lower bed of limestone, involving manual excavation of trenches 30–35ft wide and some 40ft below ground level, deepening to 60 feet where the trench crossed the former river bed and going down 260–270ft in the north and south wing trenches which cut into the valley sides. Concrete 'counterforts' or massive foundations were built into the trench and the masonry of the dam subsequently built up upon them. Concrete piers 30–40ft high were built along the centre line of the dam to provide a backbone for the masonry structure and in the early stages of the job they carried a temporary gantry on which ran two crane tracks and two tracks for wagons.

As the trench was dug the spoil was loaded into skips and the gantry mounted steam cranes lifted these and tipped them into the wagons which were run to the spoil tips for emptying. When the excavation was complete the cranes lowered concrete into the trench and placed masonry on its foundations; the mixed concrete (in 3-tons skips) and prepared stone were brought to the gantry in wagons by rail from the mixer and the stoneyard, several locomotives being engaged on this job – the plan and photographs show stoneyard and mixer on the north slope of the valley. Each crane could handle 100 skips of concrete daily. Timber for use in the concrete work was handled by the 'blondin'. The excavation commenced 24 January 1922 and was completed by October 1925. The first concrete was ceremonially mixed and placed in the trench on 17 June 1924 (this date recorded in a contemporary minute and in the engineer's report dated October 1924). The dam was to create a lake some two miles long with a capacity of 2,200 million gallons and top water level 1,054ft above sea level.

The quarry on Carle Fell

Quarrying was on a massive scale, the quarry being first opened out on the north slopes above the site (and some 400ft above the future water level) in 1923, with output (hard-grained sandstone) commencing in earnest in 1924–25. The rail lay-out in the quarry can be seen on the plan. A two roads locomotive shed was built on the main level and here were stabled ALLENBY, BEATTY, HAIG and TROTTER, when not hard at work between quarry face and incline head. An impressive and largely self-acting (i.e. balancing) incline descended to about the level of the eventual dam top. A steam winder operated a single track incline, which brought down wagons of stone from the intermediate and upper levels. A 2ft gauge track with Simplex petrol locomotive and trucks worked on removing overburden above the upper face. A two roads locomotive shed on the upper standard gauge level in the quarry was occupied by IAN HAMILTON and STRINGER during some severe winter weather when concrete could not be laid.

Near the foot of the main quarry incline was the stoneyard, where the masons worked on the stones for the dam, aided by four stone dressing machines. 100 yards to the east were the stone crushers. A Hadfield crusher with jaws 42in x 30in took pieces of up to 25cwts and they came out in 5–10lbs pieces which were reduced in two gyratory crushers (working in parallel) to suit concrete making. The concrete mixer, which also used ballast and sand from bins, was sited a little below the crushers on the hillside and from it the steel-box skips were filled for zig-zag shunting to reach the gantry above the dam. Some of the crushed stone was carried across the valley by the lower 'blondin' to another concrete mixer on the south side.

Granite was imported by rail from the Shap Granite Company's quarries – near Shap summit on the West Coast main line and this was used for the various water channels. There was also granite from Norway.

Nineteen or twenty rail-mounted and self-propelling steam cranes were used, mainly in the quarry and on the dam gantry, at the height of the work. Three steam navvies were employed in the quarry, two made by Ruston and one by Erie.

A ceremonial visit to the quarry was made on 5th June 1925. On this occasion the civic party used motor cars from the Bradford Town Hall throughout to Scar Village but from Scar platform made a zig-zag tour by train to visit the new steam generating plant (officially inaugurated by Sir James Hill, Bart.) and view the stoneyard. Then came the exciting ascent of the quarry incline in wagons fitted with transverse seats and, after inspecting the quarry (only newly opened out), the hair-raising descent in the wagons – a scene recorded photographically for the Corporation's records! Recrossing the valley by train, Alderman P L Craven (the deputy chairman) started up the concrete plant on the south side. Subsequently, the first batch of concrete from this plant was placed in the trench by Alderman Gadie (the chairman). The eventual return that day from Scar village to Gouthwaite Lodge (for tea) and Bradford, was by motor cars.

Progress – and completion – at Scar House

It is interesting to judge the pace of activity from some of the figures available –

Resident population at Scar Village

September	1923	–	1,004
August	1924	–	1,093	all accommodation occupied, numbers varying from about 800 in winter to over 1,100 in summer (when weather impeded the job less).
August	1926	–	1,135
August	1927	–	1,009
October	1928	–		housing taxed to the utmost, some men being accommodated in Middlesmoor and Lofthouse villages and, latterly, several travelling daily by motor bus from Pateley.
August (?)	1929	–	1,017
August	1930	–	696	three hostels closed by autumn 1930
August	1931	–	452
August	1932	–	173
August	1933	–	107	21 houses and one hostel open
August	1934	–	92
August	1935	–	71
August	1936	–	31	8 houses occupied; 7 pupils at school

By about September 1923 the actual workforce had risen to 700 and in 1929, about the peak, it averaged 780, falling in 1932 to about 80. In 1931 some surplus hostel buildings were sold to the Holiday Fellowship Ltd for removal from Scar and re-erection for use of ramblers. From 1 July 1933 electric lighting in the village gave place to oil lamps, presumably due to dismantling of the hydro-electric power station preparatory to its flooding. The mission church, once at Angram, was removed from Scar village in 1934 to St. Martin's in the Fields, Haworth Road, Heaton, Bradford. It was there superseded in 1955 by a fine new church but was retained as a supplementary meeting hall, until sadly destroyed by fire in 1976. The resident missioner gave up his post at Scar on 30 September 1934. The concert hall from Scar village went to Queensbury as an institute.

On the site, as the dam rose year by year through the nineteen twenties, its structure narrowed from base to top and in the later stages the working gantry above it carried two parallel railway tracks in place of four. Indeed, by Autumn 1930, the cranes were running on a single track on top of the dam wall and being fed with concrete and masonry by the 'blondin' rather than as hitherto by railway wagons loaded with concrete skips and stone. The year of the General Strike, 1926, did not stop the work but the stoppage of coal production threatened it; however, five months stocks had been built up and the locomotives, cranes, excavators and steam engines continued at work. In September 1930 Lewis Mitchell, the Corporation's engineer, resigned owing apparently to a disagreement over his acceptance of certain outside consultancy work and in December 1930 William Newlands, hitherto deputy at the Town Hall, was appointed engineer. On 24 September 1931, during a visit by the City Council, the keystones of the cills for the water overflow across the top of the dam were laid by the Lord Mayor and members of the water committee. At this stage the major engineering work was almost complete but all sense of urgency seemed to be lost and it was not until 5 July 1935 that the main overflow valve was closed for the first time to allow water to be impounded and even then only because drought threatened other sources of supply. One can only assume that the great trade depression had so reduced demand that there was no call for Scar House waters in 1931–34. Final touches were put to masonry and paintwork in the latter part of 1935, but even then the official opening was held over until 7 September 1936 – when the party travelled by road throughout from Bradford to Gouthwaite and Scar village: at 2.40 p.m. that day the Lord Mayor called on Alderman Sir Anthony Gadie, J.P., to lay a coping stone and declare the reservoir open. That year the old house which gave Scar House its name and which had housed the Allan Best family and later the resident engineer, was demolished and a new Scar House built on the far side of the valley, at the foot of the quarry incline (by then abandoned) for occupation by the reservoir keeper and to provide a boardroom for committee visits.

A subsidiary project was the tapping of the Armathwaite Gill and Howstean Beck – which streams converged and then ran out into the Nidd below Lofthouse – in order to divert their waters to run into Scar House reservoir and so extend its gathering grounds. This involved making a tunnel through the hills south of Scar. A narrow gauge line (2ft) was used by the Corporation, twelve wagons being purchased around August 1930 and two battery electric locomotives employed. Construction had actually been started in May 1929 and it is presumed to have been completed in course of the following two or three years.

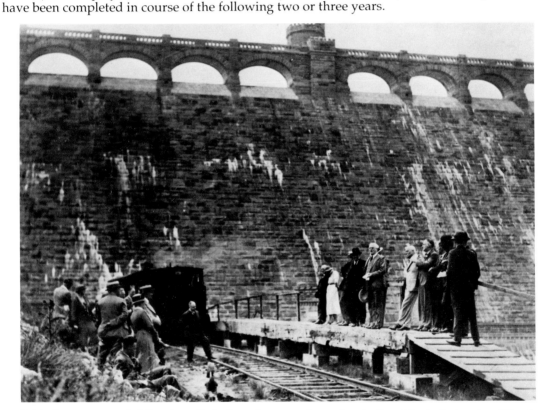

With the masonry cladding installed, the valvetower is on the skyline. The train is set well back in a temporary platform at the foot of the wall. The occasion is probably 5 July 1935, when the main overflow valve was first closed (because a drought called for use of Scar waters) – or it might be 7 September 1936, when Alderman Sir Anthony Gadie, J.P. performed the 'official opening'. Sir Anthony is speaking, notes in hand. When the huge lake is full and overflowing, the waters sweep through the arched apertures and in a vast sheet down this face. In those conditions, the surface waters can be lifted, airborne, right over the top roadway, leaving walkers dry!

L.N.E.R. No.1515 (ex-NER 'C' class, of 1889) has arrived at Pateley Bridge with a relief Sunday train, on 7 July 1935. The engine belonged to Neville Hill (Leeds) shed.

British Railways No.67253 has arrived on the early afternoon Saturday train from Harrogate, on 10 March 1951 (Sadly, the branch line closed to passengers from 2 April 1951). The loco was of N.E.R. class 'O' of 1895 and it had been the regular Pateley branch passenger engine for at least 30 years, its number being 1839 for most of its life.

Chapter Seventeen

Railway Operation in Scar House Days, 1921–1936

In the event, one former G.W.R. steam railmotor was bought – from Wake of Darlington in 1921 – and named HILL. It took over all regular passenger train working on the N.V.L.R., Pateley Bridge to Lofthouse, and is believed never to have been seen at Scar House. In 1923 it was fitted with electric light. Rolling stock was overhauled in 1921 and five of the Metropolitan coaches were turned over to workmen's use and the remainder were upholstered and painted. The coming of coaches from the Maryport and Carlisle Railway around 1922 and their accommodation with a shed at Scar site has been noted.

These carriages were presumably the ones offered for sale in November 1922, when engineer/artist David Rose journeyed from Nidderdale to Maryport to make an inspection. Twelve passenger vehicles disappeared from the operational rolling stock returns of the M & CR at 31 December 1922.

Additional locomotives, which came both new and second-hand in the early 'twenties, were mostly for site work and goods but the large six-coupled saddle tanks BLYTHE (by Avonside, 1922) and GADIE (Andrew Barclay, 1925), both painted green, were not only used as 'route engines' on through goods but were vacuum brake fitted and worked the interesting passenger trains, Scar platform to Lofthouse, and sometimes Pateley Bridge. These trains ran on Tuesdays, Thursdays and Saturdays, the first two primarily for wives and families to go shopping or visiting relatives and on Saturdays also to give the workmen themselves an opportunity of getting out of the upper Dale. The arrangements and timings varied during the years but, in general, the lighter trains run on Tuesdays and Thursdays operated from Scar platform to Lofthouse in the morning and back, respectively, around lunchtime and teatime, giving connections by the railmotor HILL over the N.V.L.R. to and from Pateley Bridge. The heavier Saturday train usually ran through to and from Pateley Bridge, leaving Scar at 1.30 p.m. and coming back from Pateley about 5.0 p.m., to reach Scar about 6.0 p.m. for tea – followed at 7.0 p.m. by whist drive and dance. Residents could reach as far as Pateley on Tuesdays and Saturdays and also Harrogate on Thursdays. This Thursday connection homeward is recalled leaving Harrogate at about 4.0 p.m. and in alternate weeks at around 6.30 p.m. A later Saturday return once a month at about 7.20 p.m. from Pateley Bridge was introduced as the demand grew and this permitted day trips as far as Harrogate, Leeds and Bradford. Excursion fares were offered from Scar to Pateley Bridge at ninepence return on three days each week. The Saturday trains were the heaviest, usually three M & CR third class coaches plus three second class vehicles. Coming back with this train, GADIE or BLYTHE was assisted from Lofthouse to Scar by another tank engine attached in rear. The Saturday trips survived longest, probably until 1932. Away back in 1920, when engineer David Rose was amongst the early residents at Scar, his daughter Margaret Rose recalls with pleasure travelling to Lofthouse on 'the loco', with a delightful smell of hot oil and various impromptu stops for sheep, passengers and water. Then a truck with wooden seats was attached and a little later the 'Black Maria' or horsebox with four little windows high up and benches round a central stove. On coming of the M & CR carriages it was accepted that certain people travelled first class and were ceremonially locked in at Scar and Pateley. Once, when there was a strike emergency, Margaret Rose, due back at boarding school, and accompanied by some members of the Addison family who had been visiting relatives at Scar, rode all the way from Scar to Pateley Bridge on a 'bogie', employing the power of gravity.

Corporation special trains were occasionally run for visiting parties, usually from Lofthouse to Scar village and Angram and back at a modest charge. The evidence is that no through excursion trains were run from the N.E.R. notwithstanding that the N.E.R. Appendix to working timetable 1922, makes provision for N.E.R. four and six wheeled vehicles and bogie vehicles not over 52 feet long to run to Lofthouse. Running of N.E.R. coaches beyond Lofthouse was specifically forbidden, as was all running of N.E.R. locomotives on the Corporation railway.

Although no through passenger trains from the waterworks railway to the North Eastern Railway were run, a notable annual event during the earlier summers from, probably, 1923, was the Sunday School outing from Scar House to Scarborough. Departure from Scar village was at 6.0 a.m., in a special train to Pateley Bridge Nidd Valley station, with a walk to the North Eastern station, then in through carriages by N.E.R. train via Harrogate and York to reach Scarborough around 11.0 a.m. On the return journey the arrival at Scar village was between 11.0 p.m. and midnight. All the village children made the trip, along with some grown-ups. The weather was usually either blazing hot or teeming with rain. Invariably, when the time for departure from Scarborough approached, some children were missing and there was a panic search for them. In some of the later years of Scar village the Sunday School outing was by 'charabanc' to Blackpool and conventional by comparison with the large scale pilgrimages to the east coast.

The passenger timetable of the N.V.L.R., in summer 1927. Interesting is inclusion of trains for workers, and families, between Scar Village and Pateley Bridge, these not being a true N.V.L.R. operation.

BRADFORD CORPORATION.

NIDD VALLEY LIGHT RAILWAY.

SERVICE OF TRAINS
From 11th July, 1927
until further notice.

PATELEY BRIDGE and LOFTHOUSE

	A.M.	A.M.	P.M.	P.M.	P.M.
Pateley Bridge	8-30	10-20	1-30	3-30	5-30
Wath	8-35	10-25	1-35	3-35	5-35
Ramsgill	8-48	10-38	1-48	3-48	5-48
Lofthouse	8-55	10-45	1-55	3-55	5-55
Lofthouse	9-10	11-0	2-30	4-10	6-10
Ramsgill	9-15	11-5	2-35	4-15	6-15
Wath	9-25	11-15	2-45	4-25	6-25
Pateley Bridge	9-30	11-20	2-50	4-30	6-30

SCAR VILLAGE and PATELEY BRIDGE.

*Scar Village   (Tuesday) 8-30 a.m. (Thursday) 8-30 a.m. (Saturday) 1-40 p.m.
*Pateley Bridge (do.) 9-30 ,, (do.) 9-30 ,, (do.) 2-20 ,,
*Pateley Bridge (do.) 1-30 p.m. (do.) 5-30 p.m. (do.) 5-15 p.m.
*Scar Village (do.) 2-30 ,, (do.) 6-20 ,, (do.) 6-0 ,,

TOWN HALL, BRADFORD.   BY ORDER,
                                LEWIS MITCHELL,
                                        Engineer.

*These trains are for the exclusive use of Scar Village residents.

The N.V.L.R., the statutory Light Railway of the Bradford Corporation, turned in passenger traffic figures as under –

Year	Workmen	Ordinary passengers	Remarks
1921	106,216	41,051	Workmen travelling in from Pateley daily
1922	24,926	38,054	Housing now at Scar village
1923	–	63,020	
1924	–	61,702	
1925	–	59,790	
1926	–	58,397	
1927	–	54,737	
1928	–	52,282	
1929	–	43,079	
1930	–	24,906	Nine months to 31/12/1929

The 1929 figures are quoted as made up for 12 months to 31/3/1929. The earlier years' returns are in annual reports dated October, but it seems to be implied that all represent 12 months to 31 March of the year in question.

Likewise, it is believed that financial statements were made up annually to 31 March, although appearing in the October reports. The aggregate net loss on the N.V.L.R., 1908 to 1924, was £36,435, the only year in that period which showed a profit being 1912. From 1925 profits were the rule –

1925	net profit	£1,323
1926	net profit	£1,141
1927	net profit	£790
1928	net profit	£1,477
1929	net profit	£693
1930	net loss	£1,825

Line closed to public passenger and goods traffic on 31 December 1929.

The net figures quoted are arrived at after deducting interest on loans, also depreciation and other accounting adjustments.

Changes amongst the staff of the Light Railway were infrequent. In January 1928 the stationmaster at Lofthouse, who had served on the line in various capacities for twenty years, was suspended consequent on 'irregularities' affecting the takings and was demoted. Then, on 6 February 1929 Ted Fawcett, stationmaster at Pateley Bridge N.V.L.R. since the beginning, died; a note of appreciation describes him as conscientious, trustworthy and efficient.

By the spring of 1929 motor bus competition between Pateley and Lofthouse was worrying the Corporation and the N.V.L.R. fares were reduced from 9d single and 1/6d return to 6d and 1/- (and 9d return on Thursdays and Saturdays). At the same time, a committee meeting at Gouthwaite Lodge, 12 April 1929, resolved to take preliminary steps to close the N.V.L.R. to public passenger traffic. First, the London and North Eastern Railway were approached but Mr Hornsby, divisional general manager, declined to take over the N.V.L.R. and its stock in view of the road competition in the district. The L.N.E.R., North Eastern Area, dependent on coal and heavy industry on the Tees and the Tyne, was particularly hard hit by slump and also by a multiplicity of private motor bus operators and, in 1929–31, discontinued various branch passenger services of their own. In consequence, the N.V.L.R. closed to public passenger service on 31 December 1929 and public goods traffic was also discontinued. The line continued in being as a private railway, not requiring Parliamentary sanction, and the distinction between the line below and above Lofthouse was lost. The substitute journey from Lofthouse to Pateley by West Riding bus was a rough one down the winding road.

Mr Humphrey Household (see Preface) explored the route to Scar enthusiastically on free Saturday afternoons. This group of views from 1928 is presented as a tribute to his success in capturing the scenes and atmosphere:–

MILNER of 1909 heads an 'ordinary train' at Lofthouse station, facing up-valley. The NVLR passenger service, Pateley Bridge–Lofthouse, was still running but was withdrawn after 31 Decr. 1929.

Freight for Scar site, with cement probably predominant, climbs the bank above Lofthouse. Six-wheel coupled locomotives MILNER (HC 882/1909) and BLYTHE (AE 1894/1922) are in front, with (believed) KITCHENER (Peckett 939/1902) and WATSON (HC 1197/1916) in rear.

The south portal of the tunnel, which dated from circa 1920 and was primarily for ascending trains, and the old route retained round the headland, for descending traffic.

BLYTHE hauls ex-Maryport & Carlisle Railway carriages on a Saturday special for residents, from Pateley Bridge homeward to Scar Village, is climbing just above the tunnel, the track from New Houses coming down across the line.

Rather remarkably, the line beyond Scar dam to Angram, although relatively inactive, had survived and it bridged the southern wing trench and southern end of the dam construction works at Scar. By June 1932 the dam had risen above the line and a narrow gap was left for it to pass through. This gap was finally built up in 1933 and that was the end of the railway to Angram, which on 3ft and then standard gauge dated back to 1904.

In the year 1936 the whole railway, Scar House to Pateley Bridge N.V.L.R. station and exchange sidings, was lifted, plant from Scar site having been brought down to Pateley Bridge. On 1 March 1937 the plant, buildings and railway track were reported to have been sold in one lot (to Maden and McKie, from Merseyside?) and on 31 March 1937 the agreement with the L.N.E.R. for connection and sidings at Pateley Bridge was terminated. The staff of the N.V.L.R. were given notice. Their jobs were not pensionable but the Corporation granted pensions forthwith to G Pearson, the locomotive driver, aged 66, with 30 years' service as driver on the N.V.L.R. and to J Brown, platelayer, aged 73, with 20 years' service. Pensions were also to be paid on attaining 65 years of age to D Thompson, platelayer, with 26 years' service, and J Storey, loco fireman, with 24 years' service; these men were aged 63 and 60 at the time of closing.

Scar village school was closed by the West Riding County Council on 31 January 1938 and later that year the vacant station offices at Pateley Bridge and Lofthouse were converted to houses. These, and the station buildings at Wath and Ramsgill, still survive and Ramsgill, complete with lawns on the ramp, platform and track bed, is a particularly pleasant house.

Even during the height of work at Scar, the letting of shooting rights over the Corporation's water gathering grounds had been a major interest – presumably profitable – and now the beautiful dale and its wild surroundings relapsed into peace not broken by the sounds of engineering construction works or the cement trains climbing the winding 'main route' with two engines in front and two behind!

Nearing Scar House, BLYTHE has a train on the road into the workshops yard; wagons of N.E.R., S.M.J.R. and L & N.W.R. appear. The Corporation (but not N.V.L.R.) main route locomotive shed at Scar is seen.

Chapter Eighteen

Locomotives in Nidderdale, distinguishing John Best and the Corporation of Bradford

Locomotives, 3ft gauge, of John Best & Son, on Angram project

TULLIBARDINE/EILEEN 0-4-0 Saddle tank oc 9in x 17in
by Andrew Barclay 297 of 1887.
It was new to Ireland & Company, Paisley for River Cart navigation works. It became Best's property and worked for him on Cowgill reservoir, near Biggar, in 1896–98; it was subsequently on his Struan job in 1899, doubling the Highland Railway above Blair Atholl, where it would secure the name TULLIBARDINE. Next assignment was Best's contract for the Cork, Blackrock & Passage Railway in Ireland (conversion of 5ft 3in gauge to 3ft gauge and extension to Crosshaven – recalled to me there as TULLIBARDINE); this work occupied the loco by 3/1900 until at least the end of 1902. *Maybe* it worked briefly on Drumbowie reservoir, Denny (Stirlingshire) around 1903–04. However, it reached Angram in 1904 with the name TULLIBARDINE (recalled to me as such); this name figures at Angram in the Best inventory of 27/12/1906, shown as a standard gauge locomotive, but I regard this gauge entry as an error. At Angram, TULLIBARDINE was renamed EILEEN.
Later: the loco went on by 1911 to Best's Delph reservoir contract (Bolton, Lancashire) and worked for the family firm there until at least 10/1913. Later again, spares for AB 297 were ordered in 3/1919 for the North Eastern Pitwood Association Ltd, of Newcastle upon Tyne, to be sent to Wynyard station, North Eastern Railway; presumably the work was in the woodlands of the neighbouring estates. The loco was heard of again – 'via Stockton-on-Tees' – in 1922.

WHITTLE DEAN/ANGRAM 0-4-0 Saddle tank oc 10in x 16in
by Hudswell Clarke 397 of 1892
Originally property of Newcastle & Gateshead Water Company at Whittle Dean reservoir above the Tyne valley, with the name WHITTLE DEAN. It was acquired by John Best and recalled to me on his Irish job, coming thence to Angram still as WHITTLE DEAN, but soon renamed: ANGRAM (no other details) was shown as a 10in loco at Angram site, 27/12/1906.
It went in 1908, or rather later, to the Delph (Bolton) contract of Bests and was known there as 'No. 21'. It was with the War Department in 1917–18; then in 1920 at Beaufort (Ebbw Vale), with contractor Brodie, as REINDEER; then with Barnsley Corporation at Scout Dike as BARNSLEY; finally with Richard Baillie at Ladybower, Derwent Valley Water Board works, being dismantled there by 1938 and gradually disappearing. Reference to the last two sites appears in *Reservoir Railways of the Yorkshire Pennines* (page B65) and *Manchester and the Peak* page 102. It was evidently nominally REINDEER to the end.

CROSSHAVEN/BUNTY 0-4-0 Wing ('inverted saddle') tank oc 8in x 12in by W G Bagnall 1480 of 1896.
New to John Best as CROSSHAVEN in 9/1897 and probably worked on his C.B. & P.R. contract from circa 9/1897 until 1904, then coming to Angram. The name BUNTY was probably acquired about the time of coming, certainly it figures in the inventory of 27/12/1906 with this name and as a 3ft gauge loco. Best ordered spares for this loco until at least 16/9/1907 but by September 1908 Sir John Jackson Ltd were ordering spares for it and it was presumably on the Kinlochleven project

139

John Best's 3ft gauge loco ANGRAM (HC 397/1892) reappears here, with, seemingly, liquid refreshment for Angram site canteen, and the saloon KITTY.

John Best's s.g. loco MIDGE probably being AB 688/1891.

of 1907–10 in the West Highlands as Jacksons' property – as it was listed in their catalogue of surplus locos lying at Grays in 1921.

Later again, it worked for P & W Anderson Ltd, still as BUNTY and numbered 36 in their time, building the North Devon and Cornwall Junction Railway, which was opened by the Southern Railway in 1925.

PENICUIK/THE NIDD 0-4-0 Wing tank oc 8in x 12in

by W G Bagnall 1423 of 1893 was new to J & M Hawley as FLYING ROCKET and evidently used during construction of Grimwith reservoir for Bradford Corporation, a site discussed in the present story under 'Projects carried out or designed prior to 1863', the small locomotive working, so it seems, during 1893–96. By 10/1897 Bagnall 1423 figures with John Best, illustrated in 1901 as THE DUKE on his work near Penicuik installing the aqueduct for Edinburgh from the Talla reservoir.

PENICUIK on 3ft gauge is a loco listed as at Angram in Best's inventory dated 27/12/1906 and one deduces that this was the one time THE DUKE from Penicuik way. Its next name would seem to be THE NIDD but this is deduced from the records of the later owner for Bagnall 1423, namely Sir John Jackson Ltd, who had it in 1908, doubtless on the Kinlochleven job of 1907–10, and who listed it as THE NIDD Bagnall 1423 for disposal at Grays in 1921.

It should be added that the name of NIDD was recalled to me as a Bagnall-built narrow gauge loco (not to be confused with Holme and King's NIDD) by an old friend who worked with Best in Nidderdale from 1906 (at age of 15 years) until 1915; I think this 'composite' account of Bagnall's 1423 is proven on most counts.

FIREFLY   0-4-0 Saddle tank oc 6in x 12in

by Black Hawthorn of Gateshead 252 of circa 1873.

Formerly at Butterknowle Colliery, near West Auckland, County Durham, where it was offered for sale at 26/7/1910 and presumably purchased by the Bests and brought to Angram.

Later, it went on to Delph (Bolton) for Bests by the autumn of 1913, passing to Lanark County Council, Camps, near Crawford circa 1917 and sold probably for scrapping in 1940.

The existence at site of FIREFLY was not generally recalled by my informants contemporary with Best's work there; however, Mr Middlemiss recalled it, unprompted, with this name and as built by Black Hawthorn; he visualised it on the remote north bywash construction, upstream of the dam on the 'far' bank and one notes that its sojourn at Angram would not exceed three years, and this quite late in the era of construction.

The names BUNTY and EILEEN were after daughters of John Best. The other names are self-explanatory. It will be found that most of the standard gauge locomotives of the Best era only carried numbers in the firm's stock. They are discussed hereafter.

One 3ft gauge locomotive figured in Best's sale in Nidderdale in 1920 (along with one standard gauge loco) but it is not apparent that it could be any one of those listed above.

No. 12 (possibly)	MIDGE (painted)	0-4-0 Saddle tank oc 13in dia. by Andrew Barclay 688 of 1891

(later, at AB's works, 'Rebuilt 1912' and later again 'Rebuilt 1946' under AB's name).

AB 688/1891 was new on 1/5/1891 to the Clyde Navigation Trust in the construction era of Cessnock (later, Prince's) Dock, Govan, job of 1886–97; passed by 2/1899 to John Best, evidently on his long-running docks construction works at Leith, and still located at Leith at 27/12/1906 (then identified in an inventory solely as 13in cylinder loco MIDGE by Barclay). MIDGE was recalled to me as on site at Angram: quoted as 0-4-0ST by AB, 'a big loco, comparable with GAMESHOPE'.

A new boiler (for AB 688) was ordered in 5/1911 by Bests from their Edinburgh address, the loco's then location not quoted, and a 'Rebuilt 1912' plate was acquired.

Later: (stated by an Angram source) MIDGE was with Braithwaites Sand and Gravel Company, Stourton, Leeds (alt: Leeds Sand and Gravel Company).

The loco (i.e. AB 688) was with Armstrong Whitworth & Co. Ltd, Newcastle upon Tyne, in their busy first world war period, with plates 'No. 15' on the cab upper panels, presumably fitted there. It passed to Steetly Lime and Basic Co. Ltd, Coxhoe; it was there until broken up late in 1959, complete with plates AB 688/1891 and 'No. 15', also ones recording its rebuilding in 1946 by AB – but the cylinders differed from those of Nidderdale MIDGE. There thus remains a niggling reservation on the identity of MIDGE, until such time as a precise record of the engine's rebuildings is discovered.

No. 13 (stated to be unnamed) 0-4-0 Saddle tank oc – recalled from Angram to be built by Andrew Barclay and to be 'high wheeled' and quite a big engine, but with hand brake only.

'No. 13' is shown as at Angram on 27/12/1906, but without other details.

The identity may well be *Andrew Barclay 241 of 1882, 11in cylinders*; that loco was new 7/2/1882 to Burntisland Oil Co., who ordered spares in 11/1887 but who closed down a few years later. It was used by Best on his Highland Railway extension contract, Strome Ferry–Kyle of Lochalsh, job of 1893–97, and was there by 8/1896; also on his C.R. construction, Connell Ferry–Ballachulish (of 1898–1903) and was on this project by 6/1899 and until at least 10/1902, with spares ordered intermediately in 9/1898 under the address of Leith Docks.

'No. 13' was at Angram by 27/12/1906 (inventory) but with no dimensions or maker quoted.

Best ordered spares for AB 241/1882 (quoted with 11in cylinders) in 8/1918 (from his Edinburgh address but not stating the loco's location) *and in 4/1920 specifically for his Angram contract, via Pateley Bridge*. This implies that AB 241/1882 was the solitary *standard gauge* loco of Best's offered for sale at Pateley Bridge on 22/9/1920.

One must of course treat this identification of 'No. 13' with AB 241/1882 with reserve. The loco has not been traced further as 'No. 13' nor as AB 241/1882.

No. 14 GLENCOE   0-4-0 Saddle tank oc 10in x 18in
by Andrew Barclay 723 of 1892 – new to Hugh Kennedy & Sons, contractors, and employed by them at Clydebank on part of the Lanarkshire & Dunbartonshire contract (job of 1893–96) and subsequently on their Carr Bridge route contract (of 1890–97) for the Highland Railway, located there by 5/1895 at latest. Acquired by John Best for his Connell Ferry–Ballachulish C.R. contract of 1898–1903 and there by at latest 2/1900, the name GLENCOE being given on the Ballachulish job.

	Best's inventory of 27/12/1906 lists 'No. 14' (no details given) as then on the Angram project and spares for AB 723 were ordered by Best for Pateley Bridge in 8/1909. The loco was recalled as No. 14 GLENCOE in Nidderdale.

Best's inventory of 27/12/1906 lists 'No. 14' (no details given) as then on the Angram project and spares for AB 723 were ordered by Best for Pateley Bridge in 8/1909. The loco was recalled as No. 14 GLENCOE in Nidderdale.

Later: on eventual disposal of most of Best's locos from Angram, Murdoch McNeil, usually the driver of GAMESHOPE, took one of the locos to the Glasgow district, believed to Stewarts & Lloyds Ltd. This would tally with the later owner of AB 723, which has been recorded as at Clydesdale Works, Mossend, period uncertain.

No. 15 GAMESHOPE   0-4-0 Saddle tank oc 12in x 20in
by Andrew Barclay 820 of 1898 – new circa 6/1898 to James Young & Sons as GAMESHOPE No. 17 and worked on Edinburgh Corporation's Talla waterworks for Young and later for John Best at that site. Best moved it on by 9/1902 to his Connell Ferry–Ballachulish contract for the C.R. and it was there until at least 6/1903. It evidently returned from Argyll to Talla by 5/1905, when Best had spares sent to Broughton. It may have had a sojourn (loan) with Young & Company who had spares recorded in Barclays' books to Rumbling Bridge in 10/1905, but it was recalled coming *direct* from Talla to Angram around 1905; certainly by 8/1906 it figured at Angram and in the inventory of 27/12/1906 it was No. 15 (no details given). GAMESHOPE was honoured on 11/9/1907, taking over at Lofthouse the special train (including the City of Bradford's saloon carriage) by which the Lord Mayor had just ceremonially 'opened' the Nidd Valley Light Railway from Pateley Bridge. Best's loco worked the train on through the upper dale to Angram. Spring side buffers were fitted, unlike generally comparable Barclay-built locos around Angram site. Delivery of spares to Pateley Bridge, after 1906, were noted in 1907, 1910, 1912 and 1913, all for AB 820, so confirming its continued presence. A new firebox ordered for it in 8/1908 was delivered to Edinburgh but probably consigned on to Nidderdale. It was the 'route' (main line) engine on materials trains, Pateley–Angram and driven by Murdoch McNeil, uncle of Mr John Kelly, Junior, of Leeds. Billy Kerr, of Leeds, told me he thought he saw it at Devonport when embarking in the first war for Mesopotamia. It is believed it went from Angram to Edinburgh, by 1914, before its disposal by Best.

Many later owners: including H W Johnson & Company, of Rainford, Lancashire (by 5/1918); W Vernon & Sons, millers, of Seacombe, Birkenhead; Cudworth & Johnson of Wrexham, engineers and dealers (probably prior to its resale circa 1926 to George Wooliscroft, Etruria, their ETRUSCAN); it was purchased by Joseph Perrin & Son, Birkenhead, providers of rail transport, and reached them on 11/11/1950 direct from Etruria – it was soon named PERRIN and as such was a familiar sight operational on Merseyside until at least 1962.

(NB: no loco No. 16 figures at Angram)

No. 17 JIM   0-4-0 Saddle tank oc 10in x 18in
by Andrew Barclay 754 of 1895 – new to Scots contractor Charles Brand & Son and employed building the branch from the Great North of Scotland Railway, extending from Ellon to Cruden Bay and Boddam, job of 1893–97; the loco was probably there until 6/1897, when a sale was held. It passed to John Best, seemingly in 6/1897, initially at Leith, subsequently on the Connell Ferry–Ballachulish job of 1898–1903, where it acquired the name JIM (by 1900). A photograph on that job, believed to be of this engine with rather faint inscription in the tank paintwork, includes a four-wheeled 'loco tender' lettered '17' (this attachment being a truck or bogie attached in the Scots tradition, to carry additional fuel – and the rope-runner or shunter).

Arrival of this loco on the Angram job was said to be from Best's Penicuik yard (Would it be from Talla? or even Leith?). It was described in Nidderdale as No. 17 LITTLE JIM but is illustrated simply lettered JOHN BEST No. 17. I was told that it was an Andrew Barclay loco smaller than GAMESHOPE.

In the inventory of 27/12/1906, under Angram, the entry is 'No. 17 with bogie' (which might be the 'engine tender' or indicate confusion with 0-4-4 Tank engine No. 19).

Spares for AB 754 were ordered by John Best for Pateley Bridge in 4/1907, 7/1907 and 8/1909.

The loco AB 754 was rebuilt by Andrew Barclay in 1912.

Later: It reached Gavin Paul & Sons Ltd at Vogrie Colliery, Fushiebridge, certainly there in 9/1918, probably superseded in earlier 1920s and with Wood & Company of Old Teapot Brickworks, St. Helens in Lancashire; and then to their successors, J J Bate & Son Ltd, and surviving there until at least 1939.

It is felt that available illustrations support the continuity of the foregoing story and the identity of the locomotive.

John Best's No.17, also known as JIM, believed to be AB 754/1895.

No. 18   0-4-0 Saddle tank oc by Andrew Barclay, said to be named, was recalled in Nidderdale on the Angram project, as 'a big engine'. JOHN BEST No. 18 is listed in the inventory of 27/12/1906 as then at Seaton Carew and being a 12in loco. A photograph reproduced depicts it at Angram and supports this title and the cylinder dimension of about 12in diameter. The picture suggests an early locomotive but with a later (e.g. turn-of-century) tank fitted. The earlier history and identity of this loco present a problem. It may be justified to identify the two following descriptions as being of the same engine, and that engine being JOHN BEST No. 18.

0-4-0 ST oc 12in cylinders AB 197 of 1879, supplied originally to Edinburgh contractor John Waddell and believed used by them on works at Newmarket, job of 1877–79; acquired by John Best, Leith, by 9/1897 and at New Dock, Leith in 5/1902 (when AB's boilermakers attended to repair the boiler), and there to at least 10/1902.

0-4-0 ST oc rebuilt by AB at their Kilmarnock Works, for John Best, and allocated REBUILT No. 9070. At 30/4/1898, the internal instruction was to send out the loco 'early next week, painted claret with JB on the tank' (implying a special interest by John Best, Senior). At 11/5/1898, under 9070, the Barclays entry was, for John Best, Leith, 'Repairing 12in loco £458' (a substantial sum in those days). At 13/2/1899, further firebox work was noted by the makers as part of the 'rebuilding' and, curiously, at 1/11/1899, the record indicated that AB were still 'rebuilding' under 9070 for the Leith address.

Bests had spares ordered 24/1/1912 for 9070 but with no destination recorded by Barclays.

A loco No. 9070 figured at Darlington & Simpson Rolling Mills Co. Ltd, their No. 2, but was seemingly superseded by a new No. 2, delivered 1943.

John Best's No.18, an early loco of clear Scots antecedents

No. 19 (known in Nidderdale as 'J.B.') 0-4-4 Side tank ic 18in x 26in by Hudswell Clarke 612 of 1902 – new 4/1902 to John Best as No. 19 and delivered via Broughton C.R. station – for Best's Talla contract. It was the 'main line' locomotive employed between Broughton and the site well up Tweeddale.

It came from Talla to Angram but did not take kindly to the curves in Nidderdale and was largely restricted to trips between the foot of Best's quarry incline near Scar House and Angram site, driven by David Cockburn.

The inventory of 12/1906 lists only 'No. 17 with bogie', as already mentioned, quoting Angram location, but this may confuse two locomotives.

Later: with Sir W G Armstrong Whitworth & Co. Ltd on Tyneside – and from 1919 with the Lilleshall Company in Shropshire; broken up in 1934.

No. 20 WARRISTON	0-4-0 Saddle Tank – by Black Hawthorn, whose number may be 568, with a one-time history at a Birmingham gas works, leaving there in the 1890s and becoming a John Best loco. It was named after John Best's house in Edinburgh. The inventory of 27/12/1906 shows loco WARRISTON at Angram. I was told that it sometimes shared a shed with No. 19, at Angram. In 1910–11 Mr Charles Johnson, later of Leeds, looked after a pump which kept the excavations at Angram clear of water and in emergencies WARRISTON was used as a boiler to supply steam to this pump – which implies a rather run-down old engine. (By the time of the Delph contract, Best No. 20 was HC 424 of 1897, a narrow gauge loco, which is thought to have reached Delph site at Bolton around 1908.)
MOLLY	0-4-0 Saddle tank. No maker has been identified. It had a square tank and weatherboard, no covered cab – but an extempore cab was contrived of timber and corrugated iron; the description given could fit the old loco seen in a picture which accompanied my account of Best's work at Talla, indeed MOLLY was said to have been brought from Talla. MOLLY came to Angram some years after the job started, and one informant dubbed her 'a little farce'. She occasionally staggered around on site with two skips of concrete or took a turn working spoil to the tips, but the boiler was negligently lit up without water and ruined – so the loco was laid aside. Mr Kelly recalled that he and other boys would play with it; his finger remained scarred where nearly cut off by a friend operating the cylinder cocks. It was broken up on site. It is said to have once been in Ireland and it took me some time to discover that MOLLYDO (the name by which all recalled it) would be the Gaelic for BLACK MOLLY, and correctly spelled MOLLY DUBH! Mr R N Clements provided this helpful item of information.

So we conclude my understanding of the locomotives which John Best Senior, and his sons brought to windswept Angram to play their part on 3ft and standard gauge tracks at various times between about 1903 and 1920, although mostly during the pre-1914 years. They were quite a bunch and there is still much to discover about them individually.

Locomotives, all standard gauge, property of Bradford Corporation (and not of contractors) employed in Nidderdale on the Scar House project.

GADIE/CRAVEN	0-4-0 Saddle tank oc 14in x 20in. 3ft 7in wheels by Hudswell Clarke 1411 of 1920 – came new, being the loco on offer (from maker's stock?) to the Corporation in 3/1920 and purchased 5/1920, when the committee decided to name it after their chairman. It left the maker's works, in Leeds, on 12/5/1920, for Pateley Bridge. It was turned out by Hudswells in green, lettered (a little surprisingly) 'NIDD VALLEY LIGHT RAILWAY' on the tank, above the nameplates. The name of 'LEWIS MITCHELL, ENGINEER' appeared on the bunker, bottom corner. This GADIE has been photographed at one of the cement plants at Scar, with the waterworks committee, probably on their visit in 1925. Its nameplates were transferred to Andrew Barclay 1866 of 1925, a larger and more imposing locomotive, which was available for hauling passenger trains; the small GADIE then became CRAVEN. Its duties included trips between the stoneyard and dam at Scar. It was probably allocated to the shed on the north bank. Later owner: Bradford Corporation Gas Department – I have understood that it was moved direct from Nidderdale to Laisterdyke gas works around 12/1930, although 11/1929 has been quoted elsewhere, with apparent authority. The name CRAVEN was retained in gasworks service and it was broken up at Laisterdyke circa 4/1957.

WATSON 0-6-0 Saddle tank oc 14in x 20in. 3ft 7in wheels, Walschaerts valvegear, slidevalves above the cylinders
by Hudswell Clarke 1197 of 1916

It was new to the Ministry of Munitions (MM) Gretna factory on 15/6/1916 as their 'DES 2' in dark green, and had vacuum brake, evidently fitted at Gretna to permit working of internal passenger trains. It was in Nidderdale by 1921 and was there named WATSON, after the distinguished (chief) engineer of the Waterworks Department 1891–1919. It was a useful engine, sharing passenger work, working goods, banking, and also on heavy site duties between the concrete plant and dam at Scar; allocated to Scar Village shed. A new firebox was fitted by Kitson of Leeds. The loco was for sale in 8/1934.

Later owners: Richard Baillie, Ladybower reservoir contract for Derwent Valley Water Board, Derbyshire, 1935–45; see my *Reservoir Railways of Manchester and the Peak* p.99 for reference to this loco and also passenger carriages acquired from Nidderdale for the Ladybower job, also at p.102 but it will be seen above that the vacuum brake was fitted from before Bradford Corporation days and the loco's passenger haulage in Nidderdale took in Scar–Pateley runs, not primarily NVLR. Later again: with N.C.B., Woolley colliery, near Barnsley, disused there by 1/1964.

MITCHELL/ILLINGWORTH 0-6-0 Saddle tank oc 14in x 20in. 3ft 7in wheels, Walschaerts valvegear, slidevalves above the cylinders
by Hudswell Clarke 1208 of 1916 – new to MM, Gretna 19/6/1916, their 'DES 3' in dark green, and having vacuum brake at Gretna, like the preceding engine DES 2/WATSON.

Arrival in Nidderdale was by 1922 and it was there named MITCHELL, after the (chief) waterworks engineer, 1920–1930, who succeeded after James Watson's death. MITCHELL was allocated to Scar Village and employed on various duties, generally parallel with those of similar engine WATSON; clearly recalled on Saturday passenger trains, Scar House–Lofthouse or Pateley and return, and weekday concrete trips on the dam site. Renaming probably followed the resignation in 1930 of Lewis Mitchell, the Corporation's engineer, but was a discourtesy to him. At the same time, Councillor (later Alderman) William Illingworth of the waterworks committee was pleasantly acknowledged. For sale, 8/1934.

Later owners: Sir Robert McAlpine Ltd by 4/1937 (and Mr M Cook has ascertained that the loco passed from Bradford Corporation to makers Hudswell Clarke of Leeds 2/10/1936, received the name HAROLD (I presume after overhaul and repainting) and went on to McAlpines on 28/4/1937). I saw this engine as McAlpine No. 88 HAROLD on 29/8/1937 at the site of the huge Ebbw Vale steelworks which McAlpines were constructing for Richard Thomas and Baldwins Ltd. It was resold to Mowlems by 5/1940 and engaged 1940–41 with the name SWYNNERTON, building R.O.F. Swynnerton; then R.O.F. RUDDINGTON until 1942–43, and it was in Mowlems' Welham Green yard in 3/1943; seen by me on their Workington breakwater contract, in 5/1946. That was not the end as work followed on Mowlems' Braehead power station contract, near Renfrew, circa 1947–51, followed (directly?) by return to Welham Green, where the yard was beside the East Coast main line southward of Hatfield. By 5/1957 the loco was in the yard at West Ewell of J W Hardwick & Sons – and (in 1973?) it was in Cambridgeshire, for private preservation.

PIONEER/HAIG   0-6-0 Saddle tank ic 13in x 20in. 3ft 4in wheels
by Manning Wardle 1224 of 1891 – a design known as the maker's '13 inch special'; delivered when new with vacuum brake and – most exceptionally – with separate brake rigging and brake blocks for the hand and vacuum brakes.
Delivery was on 16/6/1891 to Logan and Hemingway, as PIONEER (painted name), at Beighton; this was on the extension of the Manchester, Sheffield and Lincolnshire Railway (later Great Central Railway) main line southwards of the Sheffield district and one knows that 'Paddy Mail' workers trains were run in course of this work, even penetrating the main line station at Sheffield Victoria as well as traversing the contractors' constructional lines. It had major repairs for Logan and Hemingway at the maker's works in 1905; again in 1907 (probably also at the Manning Wardle works) and in 1910 (general repair and new crank axle; and the boiler was sent to M.W. in 7/1914 for a new firebox). The loco was still PIONEER, then at MM, Gretna in 12/1918, having had new cylinders in 2/1918; it may then still have been the property of Logan and Hemingway but was regarded as part of the factory loco stock. PIONEER came to Bradford Corporation by 3/1921, just possibly initially at Chellow Heights (this culled from a note in the maker's register) but it was soon in the Nidd valley as PIONEER, with weatherboard (no cab), side buffers and painted name. It still had vacuum brake on coming, indeed as already noted this was fitted right back to 1891. It received the name HAIG at Scar House, and was the first loco up in the quarry, allocated to the quarry loco shed and continuing to work here – no call there for vacuum braked stock! The cab was soon well boarded up against the elements. For sale 8/1934.
Later owners: George Wimpey, on the London Transport Ruislip extension at Park Royal, alongside the G.W.R. Birmingham line in 5/1938. A HAIG was reported near Wolverhampton in 4/1942, maybe this loco in transit; I saw it in 8/1942 and 8/1947 at Worscliffe lime works and quarry, Conisbrough, of Yorkshire Amalgamated Products Ltd, there named EILEEN: resold circa 1949 to Crawley Russell & Co. Ltd of Doncaster – and thence to one J W Perkins?

IAN HAMILTON   0-6-0 Saddle tank oc 13in x 18in. 3ft wheels by Hudswell Clarke 480 of 1897 – new 12/2/1897 to William Shakespeare of Frodingham as TRENT No. 4, at Trent Iron Works, in dark green livery when supplied; thence probably, in 1915, via the makers to H Symington & Son, contractors, at MM, Gretna. It was shown in the MM, Gretna list of 12/1918 as 'rebuilt 1915', with the name TRENT.
The loco came to the Nidd valley as TRENT and was named after arrival IAN HAMILTON (with nameplates). It was probably at north bank shed as it was used extensively between the north concrete plant and the dam. It later had a spell at the top quarry loco shed and worked on that level.
For sale, 8/1934. I saw it in Pateley Bridge N.V.L.R. shed in 7/1935.
It was attributed by its makers to Sir Lindsay Parkinson & Co. Ltd in 9/1937, but I have failed to identify it with their sites.

The four preceding locomotives from Gretna probably arrived in the Nidd valley in 1921. Three other second-hand locomotives follow.

ALLENBY   0-6-0 Saddle tank ic 13in x 18in. 3ft wheels
by Manning Wardle 1379 of 1898: maker's ordinary class 'M' new 1/7/1898 to Price and Wills at Battle with the name SIDLEY, for building the South Eastern Railway's Crowhurst–Bexhill branch; still 'in the family' with C J Wills at Henley-in-Arden, building the G.W.R. North Warwickshire line, 1905–07; then in 1907 to Topham, Jones and Railton Ltd, Crymlyn Burrows, Swansea, as their '32' (used, maybe, building the King's Dock, Swansea, or the G.W.R. Clarbeston

Junction–Fishguard Harbour route). Subsequently it was with Easton Gibb & Son Ltd at Rosyth Dockyard on the Forth.

The loco came to the Nidd valley circa 1921 with the Easton Gibb number, thought to be '54' (but 54 was MW 1664 of 1905, at Rosyth). It was rebuilt 1921 (by the makers?), then spent most of its time up in the quarry, allocated to the quarry shed. There was a new boiler by Kitsons in 5/1932.

For sale, 8/1934. I saw it in 7/1935 in Pateley Bridge shed.

Later owners: Its sale was evidently in 6/1937 and it passed to Sir Lindsay Parkinson & Sons Ltd and worked for them in building R.O.F. Chorley, near Euxton in Lancashire, as Plant No. 206 ALLENBY of SLP, until 1939. It lay intermediately at Lostock Junction (where I viewed it in 9/1939); it soon moved to SLP's R.O.F. Risley contract, going on from there in 12/1941 via other SLP sites, reaching Leeds, 8/1943; reported at SLP's Temple Newsham yard, near Leeds, in 6/1947 and 9/1947 but gone, probably for ever, by 9/1950.

BEATTY	0-6-0 Saddle tank ic 13in x 18in. 3 ft wheels by Manning Wardle 1669 of 1905: maker's ordinary class 'M' new 30/10/1905 to Easton Gibb & Son at Dunston-on-Tyne as their No. 59 – presumably preparing the site for Dunston Power Station (which was operating in 1910) or N.E.R. developments in the area; also worked on their Newport and Rosyth contracts, still as No. 59. The loco probably came to the Nidd valley circa 1921, recalled as '59' but soon named BEATTY, with nameplates. It was employed between the concrete plant and dam at Scar, but supplied steam circa 1924 for pumping out the foot of the embankment trench; later it was stationed and worked up in the quarry. It had new cylinders in 1925. On 6/2/1926, respected observer J W Armstrong recorded it at Scar House as 'BEATTY 59'. It was rebuilt 1928: new firebox by Kitsons. For sale 8/1934. I saw it in Pateley shed, 7/1935. Later owner: Raine & Co Ltd., Steelworks, Dunston-on-Tyne, where it was received circa 1938 and where I saw it in 6/1946 and, out of use, in 4/1955. It is believed to have been broken up at Raines in 1959, having started and finished its working life in Dunston, yet having enjoyed a long and active era high above Scar House, in the dales!
KITCHENER	0-6-0 Saddle tank oc 14in x 20in. 3ft 6in wheels by Peckett 939 of 1902 – worked for Topham, Jones and Railton as 40 ABBEY and subsequently for S Pearson & Son, latterly on construction of King George V Dock, London, project of circa 1912–21. Mr Haines, who had recently joined the Bradford Corporation, brought this loco, as ABBEY, from a Darlington yard (probably that of J F Wake, the well known dealer of the period) to Nidderdale circa 1921. It was soon KITCHENER and, at Scar, worked mainly between the foot of the quarry incline and the stone crusher with stone for concrete making. Acquired a new firebox by Kitsons and (soon afterwards?) was for sale in 8/1934. In 2/1936, reported stored at Scar House. Later owner: KITCHENER has been reported sold from Nidderdale for £700 in 6/1937. It found its way to Millom and Askam Hematite Iron Co. Ltd, at Millom Iron Works, Cumberland, arriving there about 1939: their 4 KITCHENER when I saw it in 8/1946 and again in 8/1952; it still retained spring balance safety valves attached to an old-fashioned Peckett bell-mouthed dome. Believed broken up on Millom Works pier circa 1952–53.

From Scar House construction days, a 'snap' by Thomas Garth of the elusive BEATTY (Manning Wardle 1669/1905)). ALLENBY was similar.

Also for Scar House duties, ILLINGWORTH (called MITCHELL until 1930) was HC 1208/1916 and similar to WATSON (HC 1197/1916). They were to an uncommon design of Hudswells, with outside Walschaerts valve gear. Both started life at Ministry of Munitions, Gretna, in the first war, before their days as route engines for Scar site era.

Now come the four new locomotives delivered to the corporation in 1922–25:

BLYTHE 0-6-0 Saddle tank oc 14½in x 20in. 3ft 3in wheels
by Avonside Engine Company 1894 of 1922 – came new to Nidderdale, in green livery. It was allocated to Scar Village shed and worked on the main route, with materials traffic from Pateley Bridge to Scar House.
It acquired vacuum brakes (but seemingly not at once on delivery) secured electric light, with turbo generator, and was often used on Saturday passenger trains, Scar–Pateley and back.
Later owners: This loco was sold in the early 1930s (before mid-1932) to John Mowlem & Co. Ltd. Mr Haines took it on its way to them; they were building the Southampton New Docks for the Southern Railway, a contract undertaken jointly with Edmund Nuttall.
In the mid-1930s it was acquired by Amalgamated Denaby Collieries Ltd and moved direct from Southampton to Rossington Colliery, near Doncaster – being overhauled and working there until at least the mid-1960s.

GADIE 0-6-0 Saddle tank oc 14in x 22in. 3ft 5in wheels
by Andrew Barclay 1866 of 1925 – came new.
GADIE worked, like BLYTHE, on materials trains over the 'main route' and shared Saturday passengers, Scar–Pateley, and worked the saloon too. It had vacuum brake and electric lighting, but both seem to have been fitted during the loco's career in the dale. Allocation was to Scar Village shed. The nameplates were transferred from the earlier and smaller GADIE, as an honour to Lt. Colonel Anthony Gadie, JP (later, in the 1930s, Sir Anthony). Anthony Gadie was prominent from the time of the first aqueduct construction in the late 1890s right through to 'openings' on completion at Scar House in 1936; he was soon deputy chairman of the waterworks committee and then for many years its chairman, a much liked and respected figure.
The loco GADIE of 1925 was for sale in 8/1934.
Later owner: Sale of big GADIE is understood to have been via Andrew Barclay of Kilmarnock, the engine's makers, and it was acquired circa 1937 by R B Tennant Ltd, Whifflet Foundry, Coatbridge, and worked on their rather cramped industrial layout – thus being another locomotive which exchanged breezy upper Nidderdale for very different climes. The name with Tennants was MARGIE; I saw her there in 5/1956, the only loco at the works, but it was replaced by a new Sentinel upright boiler loco in 1957 and went to nearby J N Connell Ltd for scrap.

The two preceding locomotives were the 'big boys', prominent on the main route.

TROTTER 0-4-0 Saddle tank oc 10in x 18in. 3ft wheels
by Andrew Barclay 1810 of 1925 – came new – quite a small loco, which went up at once to the quarry and spent most of its Nidd Valley career there. Alderman Trotter had been a committee member since at least 1912.
Later owners: Sold probably before mid-1932, going first to Concrete Ltd, Stourton, Leeds; then Cohens of Stanningley, dealers; and sold by them circa 1934 to Monks Hall & Company, proprietors of steel rolling mills, in Warrington, where I saw this loco in 7/1940. I believe that it was still in working order there in the early 1950s but was said to be broken up in 4/1959.

STRINGER   0-4-0 Saddle tank oc 10in x 18in. 3ft wheels. Similar to TROTTER.
by Andrew Barclay 1877 of 1925 – came new, starting on quarry duties and working on both main levels at Scar quarries.
Later owner: Bradford Gas Department, Laisterdyke Works, still as STRINGER, probably going there before mid-1932; thence via Cohens circa 1939 to Tanks and Drums Ltd, also a Laisterdyke firm, where I saw the loco as MICHAEL in 12/1949.

I discount the possibility that Barclay 1878 of 1925, another four-wheeler with 10in cylinders, came to the Nidd valley but AB 1879 of 1926, similar to big GADIE, has been quoted as delivered new in 12/1926 but being returned at once to the makers and resold 1/1927 to Naworth Coal Co. Ltd, Lord Carlisle's collieries, where we knew this loco as their STEPHENSON.

The big GADIE (Andrew Barclay 1866 of 1925), with ILLINGWORTH (HC 1208/1916) – attached to traditional tip wagons. The earlier GADIE was a four wheeled Hudswell Clarke loco, which became CRAVEN.

One may add a distinctive locomotive which has been discussed in my text when writing of 'The Nidd Valley Light Railway':

MILNER 0-6-0 Side tank oc 12in x 18in. 3ft 3in wheels
by Hudswell Clarke 882 of 1909 – new 26/5/1909, acquired specifically as a passenger locomotive for the Nidd Valley Light Railway, Pateley Bridge–Lofthouse, until replaced in 1921 by the undermentioned railmotor. MILNER was then overhauled and moved to Scar Village for passenger and goods work.
It was for sale 8/1934 and its later history is detailed in the textual reference.

Note that there had been a previous MILNER, 4-4-0 Side tank oc 17in x 24in with 5ft 10in coupled wheels, discussed in the text, acquired 1905 and sold in 1914, a relatively short career, on the N.V.L.R. specifically.

To make up the 'peak' total of fifteen locomotives nominally in the Corporation's stock (Report dated 27 October 1925), the following must also be included:

HOLDSWORTH 4-4-0 Side tank oc 17in x 24in. 5ft 10in coupled wheels
by Beyer Peacock 707 of 1866 and Metropolitan Railway No. 20 until 1905. This loco is detailed in the text under 'The Nidd Valley Light Railway' and last reported as supplying steam at Scar circa 1921. It seems to have 'rusticated' in the carriage shed at Scar House for many years as it appears in the list of locomotives for sale contained in a letter of 29 August 1934 from Kitsons of Leeds (writing on behalf of the Corporation) to Earles Cement Company. Presumably HOLDSWORTH was broken up soon after this.

No.1 HOLDSWORTH, built by Beyer Peacock 707 of 1866 for the Metropolitan Railway, was acquired in 1906–07 for passenger use on the then new N.V.L.R. The scene is beside one of the early North Eastern Railway roundhouse sheds at York, the locomotive nicely painted at Neasden and on its way to Nidderdale. No.2 MILNER (BP No.1878 of 1879) was its companion.

HILL 0-4-0 steam railmotor with oc 9in x 15in and 3ft 5in coupled wheels, transverse boiler and articulated carriage with bogie, 60ft long overall, with 48 seats, and fitted with steam and vacuum brakes –

built by Kerr Stuart of Stoke, their 906 of 7/1905, and fitted to its coach at Bristol – at the Bristol Wagon and Carriage Company's premises. It was then Great Western Railway engine 0864 and car 15. The railmotor was one of a pair for the G.W.R. and had features in common with cars built by Kerr Stuart for the Buenos Aires Great Southern Railway, the Lancashire and Yorkshire Railway, the Taff Vale Railway and the Great Indian Peninsula Railway. The G.W.R. sold to Wake of Darlington in 5/1920 and Wake resold it in 1921 to the Corporation of Bradford. Electric lighting was fitted at Pateley Bridge. Mr Hill was on the waterworks committee from at least 1912, hence the name applied.

When repairs were needed, fitters came down from Scar House, as the car was specifically for N.V.L.R. passenger use – and to the best of my knowledge HILL never ventured north of Lofthouse. I saw HILL in Pateley carriage shed in 7/1935. It went for scrap, believed in 6/1937, but the trailing end of the body, with driving vestibule, still lay in the Leeds scrap yard of J Birdsall & Company (alt: Robinson and Birdsall), in 1961, its final demise being, it is believed, in the mid-1970s.

Railcar HILL by Kerr Stuart 906 of 1905, had a career with the G.W.R. until 1920 and was acquired in 1921 for passenger duties on the N.V.L.R.

A favoured livery for the Corporation's own locomotives was red, perpetuating the precedent set by the Metropolitan Railway, but green was also popular, as witness various preceding references, as well as recollections of staff.

Sales of locomotives and plant were recalled as held at Scar House around 1935–36 but the major sale was at Pateley Bridge, in June 1937, track and other materials being by then included. Locomotives GADIE (the first)/CRAVEN, BLYTHE, TROTTER and STRINGER were sold earlier.

HILL in the Corporation carriage shed at Pateley Bridge (with two passenger carriages beyond), as captured by Arthur Camwell – and the author – on 7 July 1935.

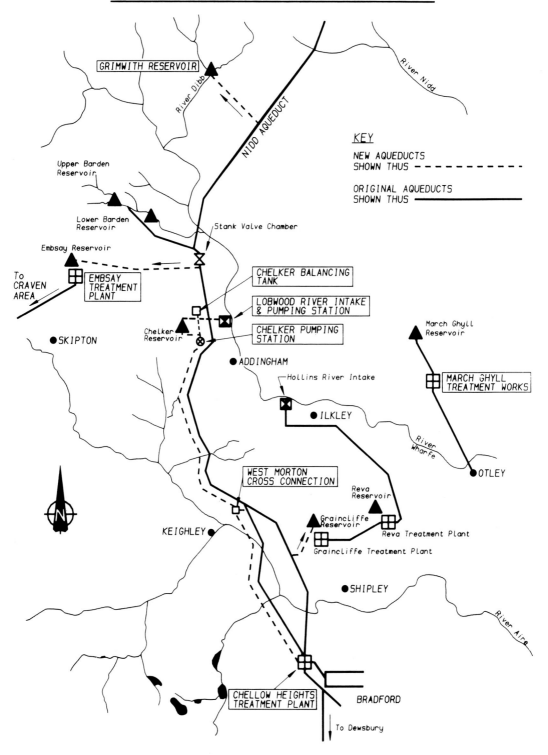

Water from the Yorkshire Dales: Addendum

The Corporations of Leeds, Harrogate and Bradford – whose reservoir construction works have been central to our story – gave place in 1974 to new local authorities. Simultaneously, their water supply works and responsibilities passed to the Yorkshire Water Authority. In 1990, one found Yorkshire Water PLC and its subsidiary companies newly constituted in place of the Y.W.A. The subsidiaries are functional, not geographical, entities.

During the later 1960s, and since, a dominant aim has been to provide ever more flexibility of sources and supplies of water, indeed moving towards a 'Yorkshire Water Grid'.

In these days, the new works involved have not called for significant constructional railways but they do focus attention on the vision and engineering achievement of such figures as Alexander Binnie and James Watson. The Nidd scheme, with initial Acts of 1890 and 1892, was executed from that time by Watson, and after his death in 1919 it was carried to completion largely as visualised in 1890, although Scar House reservoir became a single lake of much greater capacity than first intended.

I would like to publish the diagrams of 6 September 1900 (as accompanying James Watson's paper of that date) and of July 1924 (being the up-date by Lewis Mitchell incorporating Scar House reservoir in its final form). However, these do not lend themselves to reproduction so, by courtesy of Yorkshire Water PLC, I present their bolder diagram of 1990. This demonstrates how Scar House and Angram reservoirs (to be visualised 'off the top of the diagram') still feed by the Watson aqueducts to Chellow Heights, his service reservoirs in north west Bradford, and bid fair to meet much of West Yorkshire's water needs far into the 21st century.

Our overall map, found in the end covers, shows the main line railways, in the form they took around the first half of the 20th century, together with virtually all the reservoirs – thus providing a perspective.

The 1990 diagram picks up the trail at Grimwith, in moorland westward of Pateley Bridge and well north west of Bradford. Early in the present work, when touching on projects of the 1850s–1860s, Grimwith reservoir first figures; it was completed in 1864 and enlarged in the 1890s, its purpose being solely to maintain river flows for the benefit of entitled millowners. Now, its reconstruction during 1975–1983 has created an impounding reservoir with usable capacity of 4500 million gallons, at top water level of 946ft o.d., available for the first time to provide public supplies: with impounding from 18 August 1983 and formal 'opening' from 6 September 1985.

The 1990 diagram shows a new link to Grimwith, effective from summer 1990, but note that – unexpectedly, one might think – this is not initially intended for feed from Grimwith reservoir to the 'Watson' aqueduct but is to permit diversion of surplus water, as and when available, from Nidderdale to assist in the replenishment of Grimwith following a prolonged dry period. This, ingeniously, enables the maintenance of flow in the river Wharfe – to which Grimwith's waters all pass. Then, in turn, at Lobwood (downstream of Bolton Abbey and upstream of Addingham) Wharfe waters are drawn as required through the new Lobwood intake into its pumping station, completed 1980, which feeds by a new twin pipeline of about a mile to the long established Chelker reservoir.

Chelker used to feed into the aqueduct supplied from Barden, completed in 1860, which passes beneath Chelker, and so to Bradford, but now with a new pumping station installed adjacent to the reservoir, Chelker feeds a new major aqueduct, completed in 1981. This proceeds via West Morton, where a cross-connection is available to the third pipeline of the aqueduct from Nidderdale completed in 1973, to operate in parallel with the twin pipelines of the same aqueduct, previously completed in 1901 and 1921, but laid along a separate route to the west as also followed by the new aqueduct from Chelker. Onward, the Aire valley is crossed and all four lines reach Chellow Heights for treatment and distribution around Bradford and progressively through the Yorkshire Water Grid.

The Lower Barden supply route is not abandoned and at present goes by Gilstead treatment works to Heaton and Wheatley Hill (not to Chellow Heights) and so to the lower districts of

Bradford. Plans exist, however, to construct a new treatment plant at Graincliffe to replace a number of the older plants including Gilstead, and Reva (which now serves Ilkley, Guiseley and parts of Otley). These plans also include a proposal to reinforce the branch link to Graincliffe, constructed in 1975, from the Nidd aqueduct. One notes that Upper Barden, whose construction 1876–83 was discussed in the text, continues to feed by pipeline to the Nidd aqueduct, bound for Chellow Heights.

Readers may have noted from our own map, as it depicts the Bardens, Bolton Abbey and Chelker, how close Bradford's water supplies were to those secured at Embsay Moor (for Skipton), these discussed in *Lesser Railways of Bowland Forest and Craven Country*. Now, in the 1980s, a branch link pipeline has been installed giving access from the Nidd aqueduct to Embsay Moor reservoir and thus affording Craven territory the benefits of Watson's work in Nidderdale, not to mention the products of years of work by all those people and locomotives – the people and plant of Morrison & Mason, John Best and the City of Bradford.

ACKNOWLEDGMENTS

In course of my research for this work, over the years, enthusiastic help has come from many people. I am delighted to thank, among others – George Alliez, R D Allison, John W Armstrong; Allan C Baker, Mr Burrell (of 'the Greens'), Dorothy Burrows; Arthur Calvert, George Calvert, W A Camwell, Robert and Gene Cann, Mr Chadwick, Douglas Clayton, R N Clements, Eric G Cope; F K Davies, Martin Davies, Donald Dewar, Jim Dyson and Mrs Dyson; John Ellis; Mr Fenwick (stationmaster, Masham); John Garnett, Thomas Garth; J W Hague, Peter S Halton, A S Hamilton, Miss Harker, William Harris, Brian Hilton (and collection), Peter Holmes, Kenneth Hoole, Geoffrey Horsman, G N le G Horton-Fawkes, Humphrey G W Household, Hugh C Hughes, R J Hunter; Miss Ingleby; G I Jenkinson, Charles Johnson, Ivor Johnson, Frank Jux; John Kelly Junior, Duncan Kennedy, William Kerr; Lens of Sutton, Trevor J Lodge (and collection), Geoffrey Lord; Joseph McCallum, Arthur Mallaby, Mr & Mrs Fred Mallaby, E C Mark, Mr & Mrs Mason, Thomas Middlemiss, R W Miller, Edward Mills, Robert Moore, Jack Murphy; Andrew Neale; Robert B Parr, Arthur Pearson, L R Perkins, Kenneth P Plant; Stuart Rankin, Ronald N Redman, George F Renton, George Risplin, Bernard Roberts, John Robson Junior, Margaret Rose, Peter D Rowbotham, Ralph T Russell; Edward Simmons, Brian Slater, Mrs Bessie Sloan (née Miller) and Miss Miller, William J Sloan, Frank D Smith, George Smith, George H Swann, Michael Swift, Dayne Swires; A Keith Terry, C H A Townley, Simon Townsend; George Walker, Anthony Wass, Graham Watson, Russell Wear, Mr & Mrs Wilkinson, Cyril Wilson, Mr Woodrop Junior; William J Young.

Public authorities and companies:

Within the City of Leeds – the director of administration and colleagues at Civic Hall, the reference librarians at Central Library, the archivist (Mr Collinson);
Within Bradford – the administration officer (Mr Swales) of the Town Clerk's department and colleagues at the Town Hall, the local history and reference librarians and archivist at the Central Library, Bradford Art Galleries and Museums especially mentioning Miss Ann Ward, principal keeper, and Raymond McHugh, keeper of the Industrial Museum;
At Harrogate – the borough librarian and the director (Mrs P M Clegg) of museums and galleries;
Leeds Corporation Water Works department and especially Andrew S Hamilton, formerly of the head office and onetime of Colsterdale, and colleagues in the dales and distribution services;
Bradford City Water Works department and especially S Asquith (manager) and Mr Fisher (photographer) and their colleagues in the field;
Claro Water Board, Harrogate – James B Pooley (engineer) and field colleagues;
Yorkshire Water Authority (formed 1974) – W M Jollans, when director of operations, and many colleagues in Leeds head office and the field;
Yorkshire Water P.L.C. (in succession, 1990, to Y.W.A.), including Jim Crossley of Yorkshire Water Engineering Services, and P.R.O. members;
Rofe, Kennard & Lapworth, consulting engineers, of Sutton;
Andrew Barclay, Sons & Company Limited, Kilmarnock;
Hunslet Engine Company Limited, Leeds;
University of Glasgow archives;
British Railways' former archives, York;
The Public Record Office (Kew); the Scottish Record Office (Edinburgh);
The County Record Office, West Yorkshire (Wakefield); The County Record Office, North Yorkshire (Northallerton and Ripon); the ecclesiastical Parish of Masham and Healey;
The National Railway Museum.

Societies:

The Narrow Gauge Railway Society;
The Industrial Locomotive Society and its journal *The Industrial Locomotive*;

The Industrial Railway Society and *The Industrial Railway Record*;
The Stephenson Locomotive Society and its Journal.

Published works, including:

Bagnalls of Stafford (A C Baker and T D A Civil, 1973);
Contractors' Steam Locomotives of Scotland (Russell Wear and Michael Cook, published by ILS, 1990);
The Railway Foundry, Leeds (R N Redman, 1972);
The Birth and Death of a Highland Railway (Duncan Kennedy, 1971);
Navvyman (Dick Sullivan, 1983);
The Nidd Valley Light Railway (David J Croft, of Bradford City Library, 1972 and 1987);
Early Victorian Water Engineers (G M Binnie, 1981);
Illustrated Guide to Nidderdale (Thomas Whitehead, 1932);
Illustrated Rambles (James Parker);
Railway and Travel Monthly, April 1915 (Ian Rawlins);
The Railway Magazine, 1927 (A P Herbert) and other references;
Contract Journal (various entries);
Ackrill's Annual, 1905;
Yorkshire Daily Observer, 1907, and other newspapers;
Various Water Authority publications;
One hundred years of Leeds Tramways (Andrew D Young, 1970).

Arthur Chambers collaborated in the field and at his desk, preparing all the maps here reproduced, apart from the end-cover map, which is the work of David H Smith, and one from Yorkshire Water P.L.C. Douglas Rendell copied or prepared most of the photographic illustrations for publication.

H D B

(N.B. – the Author and Publisher regret that copies of photographs featured in the book cannot be supplied to individuals.)